Challenge, Comfort, Forgiveness and Welcome

Words to the World at Such a Time as This

Barry Dunsmore

Edited by Nigel J. Robb

SAINT ANDREW PRESS
Edinburgh

First published in 2007 by
SAINT ANDREW PRESS
121 George Street
Edinburgh EH2 4YN

ISBN 978-0-86153-385-5

British Library Cataloguing in Publication Data
A catalogue record for this book is available from the British Library.

It is the Publisher's policy to only use papers that are natural and recyclable
and that have been manufactured from timber grown in renewable, properly
managed forests. All of the manufacturing processes of the papers are expected
to conform to the environmental regulations of the country of origin.

Typeset in Baskerville by Waverley Typesetters, Fakenham
Printed and bound by Bell & Bain Ltd, Glasgow

Contents

PARABLES OF JESUS

CHRISTIAN LIFE

NATURE OF THE CHURCH

Preface

I have made my own selection of sermons preached by my friend Barry Dunsmore, minister of St Columba's, Pont Street, London. Some time ago, he mentioned to me that he would like me to review and edit the contents of a book of the sermons he had preached in London. Like many conversations, it noted interest and my support of the project, but it did not come to fruition for various reasons. Therefore, when the opportunity arose to celebrate not just the fiftieth anniversary of the building of the present St Columba's but also the twenty-fifth anniversary of Barry's ordination, the idea was raised again, quietly, without his knowledge.

It has been my good fortune to know and to enjoy Barry's friendship for over thirty years, since our time together as candidates for the ministry and as divinity students at Trinity College, Glasgow University. I have also had the privilege of 'preaching him in' to St Columba's, Pont Street, and participating in worship there on several occasions.

As someone who has taught the basics of preaching and biblical communication for over twenty years, I have always been interested in sermons and how they may communicate the Good News effectively and creatively. In listening to and reading Barry's sermons, I have been continually aware of his quick wit, lively mind and imaginative impulse, and of how he effectively engages and challenges his congregations.

My selection is a personal one. I have attempted to present a variety, based on my particular perspectives, and put them into various sections for ease of reference. They demonstrate the range of styles, approaches and structural designs which Barry uses in bringing his congregation 'a lively Word in Season'. I have undertaken a certain amount of editing of the texts of the sermons to make them accessible to readers. Those who know Barry as a preacher will, I trust, still hear his voice and clarity of thought.

The sermons are offered for publication in the hope that they may assist and support those who read them, and encourage them on their faith journey.

NIGEL J. ROBB
Edinburgh
Shrove Tuesday 2007

After 9/11

Words to the World at Such a Time as This

The events of 9/11 in the USA did, by all accounts, change much in the world. For the first time, the USA was attacked on its mainland, and the shockwaves and reactions were felt throughout the world. The famous 'War on Terror' was launched, and military expeditions in Iraq and Afghanistan commenced, all with long-term consequences for the citizens of this world.

Communities were affected, with suspicion of neighbours, prejudice and alarm, which were confirmed and strengthened by the events of 7/7, and subsequent warnings by senior security-service officials of the likelihood of further atrocities. Alongside these events, world poverty and hunger, injustice and domestic strife continued to impinge on the lives of millions, causing many to question and doubt the love and concern of a gracious God.

In such a situation of difficulty, doubt and change, these sermons were preached from the pulpit of St Columba's, Pont Street, London, part of the Church of Scotland. Here we see one preacher's dialogue with the Bible and with the events which were shaking and disturbing the foundations of life as people experienced unprecedented anxiety and tension in the midst of multicultural Britain.

These sermons are not timeless. They are tied to a particular set of events in a particular specific location.

Professor Edmund Steimle of Union Seminary, New York City, always maintained that any real and effective sermon must be tied to a particular time. He attacked certain of the sermons of Scottish preachers in wartime because, while they were presented in a lyrical and effective literary style, they made no allusion whatever to the fact that they were preached in wartime Britain, with congregations affected by worry, bombing, food shortages and the fear of imminent invasion. It was Professor Steimle's contention that the task of the preacher, week in week out, was to proclaim a word from heaven in a hell of a world like this.

These sermons do not evade any of the issues of this time. They are from a situation of commercial wealth and comfort, just near Harrods, in one of the major cities of this world. They avoid the temptation of offering glib and trite answers to tough questions. Indeed, they offer respect to a congregation well aware of the challenges to Christian faith in such a time as this. They articulate some of the sharp points and intense problems we have as we struggle to see good in a time of evil. They invite us to accept moral, ethical and religious responsibility in an age when these are almost incomprehensible concepts.

In this church, there is a sense of the reality of loss and the devastation of acts of war on civilians. For here, in 1941, the original church on this site was destroyed by enemy bombing. The congregation survived, grew and developed in spite of, and perhaps even because of, what happened. A distinctive and distinguished church building rose in its place and now celebrates over fifty years of Christian witness and service.

The membership, recalling the impact of the war years, and including so many friends and members with roots in the USA and connections there of business and relationship, had great empathy with the USA after 11 September 2001. In this congregation, no-one was allowed to believe that the events across the Atlantic had nothing to do with how they lived their lives or how they expressed their faith. Indeed, this church has continued to grapple with the impact of what happened since that fateful day. The congregation has been called to reflect on the multicultural dimensions and many interests which impinge on how the church remains faithful to a gospel of love and service in a world racked by hate and alienation.

Here the reader will find no assertion of theological dominance, but honesty in exploring what role the Church and Christian disciples have to play in this post-Christian and multifaith world. The varied backgrounds of the congregational members are acknowledged so that those who read these sermons will come away believing that some of their particular issues and perspectives have been addressed seriously and sensitively. The reader will find himself or herself asked to ponder areas of responsibility for the environment, poverty, justice, the homeless and the marginalised, and their personal implications. Here we are confronted with the central belief of the preacher that the gospel impacts on all aspects of life.

While the sermons were preached in a Church of Scotland congregation in London, they are not exclusive in their address or influence. Instead, they demonstrate the commitment of one preacher to take the Bible seriously, while valuing the experience and insights of his congregation's life and witness. All of them demonstrate a critical and analytical involvement with real issues.

Each preacher brings his or her life to the experience of preaching – and Barry Dunsmore is no exception. His particular hermeneutical approach (or rather, the means where he interprets and applies this message of the Bible to modern life) is a result of his training, his ministerial experience and his broad sympathies. He demonstrates throughout these reflections on God's Word a deep desire to wrestle with the real issues of living in a world when, to do so as a Christian, is countercultural, liable to misinterpretation, misrepresentation and abuse.

The sermons are reflections of Barry Dunsmore's personality. They are lively, personal, warmed by good humour and often sharp in wit and wisdom. He brings us 'truth through personality', reflecting his own perspectives as he offers rigorous debate and earthly reality. In his own distinctive way, he has fulfilled the remit given to him (quoted in the final sermon of the book) by his former supervisor :

> 'Challenge people, comfort people, forgive people, welcome people, but do not ever bore them. You have been entrusted with a message that is for the salvation of all.'

NIGEL J. ROBB

Introduction to the Preacher

I first met Barry Dunsmore in June 2000, when I was a member of the Vacancy Committee. That was a formal meeting, with him being interviewed by twenty-five of us at the same time as he, in his very direct, personal way, asked questions of us. Those questions were answered, and we duly called him to St Columba's. I next met him in July 2000 when he and his family, and I and mine, were holidaying in the USA and we literally ran into each other all those thousands of miles away. That was my first glimpse of the very human, honest, down-to-earth man of God whom we have all come to know since then.

Barry joined us in November 2000, at a lovely service where he was preached in by his great friend Nigel Robb, to whom grateful thanks are due for bringing this volume to life. Seven years on, there is a huge sense of renewal, of meeting new challenges and, positive change in the congregation of St Columba's. Worship is uplifting with Barry's outstanding preaching – always important, always topical and never afraid to address difficult issues or to recognise differences between people. The feeling of fellowship within the congregation is strong and has been greatly enhanced by the events of 2006, our fiftieth anniversary year.

For those of us who have had the privilege of getting to know Barry better, we know him to be an outstanding and loyal friend, a great support and comfort in times of need, but also a real person, with an unsurpassable capacity for humour and warmth, and very broad shoulders, which have come into play when needed, both for others and to carry his own burdens. These sermons give a flavour of that, although they will naturally lack the sometimes theatrical and awesomely perfect delivery from the pulpit. I hope you enjoy them as much as we have enjoyed hearing them, and hope to continue doing so for many years to come.

CATRIONA SUTHERLAND-HAWES
Deputy Session Clerk, St Columba's Church
Pont Street, London

September 11

16 September 2001

1 Timothy 1:12–17; Luke 15:1–10

Fourteen months ago, I stood with my family at the top of the World Trade Center in New York, and we marvelled at Manhattan. It fired the enthusiasm of our daughter even more to go and live in America – and, as you know, now she is in Washington. I take the opportunity to thank members and friends who enquired after her well-being on Tuesday night, and we were glad to say she is well. In her school, 90 per cent of the children have parents who work in Washington, 25 per cent of the parents work in the Pentagon, and some of Jenny's classmates have lost parents. So, too, it is here in the Church today. It brings it all very close:

- We have several American families in our church, some of whom are with us this morning, who work for companies which have offices in the World Trade Center and who have lost colleagues. It brings it all very close.

- We have members of this congregation recently returned to live and work in New York, to work in offices in the World Trade Center. It brings it all very close.

- We have members of this congregation, who are present this morning, who work for companies which have offices in the World Trade Center and who have lost colleagues. It brings it all very close.

The first thing we want to recognise is the human dimension to this tragedy. I heard the other night that the insurance world thought that the worst possible world scenario for them was two jets colliding over Manhattan – and we have managed to surpass even that. The human dimension of this tragedy has been heightened beyond bearing by the fruits of modern technology:

- Mobile-phone calls from within the World Trade Center and within the aircraft before they hit the buildings,
- Graphic pictures of the second aircraft flying into the building,
- the subsequent collapse of the towers,
- the rescue and the death of so many firefighters and rescue workers.

Whatever we say this morning, there is no escaping the enormous human dimension to this tragedy. Whatever else we go on to say does not in any way try to diminish that:

- as we recognise the enormous loss of life,
- as we remember those who will be permanently scarred because of injury, or being a part of the emergency services,
- or because of their experiences.

We think first and foremost of the human dimension of this tragedy.

However, there is also a political dimension to this tragedy. It has often been said that the strength of a good investment portfolio is how well it performs when the market is bad and not when the market is rising. Equally, I expect the sign of a good politician, or a world leader, is how they react in times of difficulty and tragedy, and not in times of buoyancy and growth. It is a global problem and it will require a global cooperation, if there ever is a solution.

One politician said that the world is now a different place – and yet, with Lockerbie and Dunblane, have we not been here before? Is the difference perhaps one of scale? I suspect not. I suspect the world is a different place. When we try to seek dialogue or understanding, or negotiation, we can no longer play the deterrent card that we will retaliate. We are faced with people who are prepared to kill themselves before we kill them, in causes that perhaps we scarcely begin to understand. To be told that this is the first war of the new century is not helpful, however understandable.

There is a political dimension to this tragedy, and the call is for justice, not for vengeance. Justice is no enemy to the gospel. Calling people to take full responsibility for their actions is no enemy of the gospel. Remember we seek justice, which is not the same as vengeance. Any justice that comes will require international cooperation, and the challenge for that now is that we live in a world where there are no longer any shared values, and there are no longer similar world-views, if there ever were.

The biblical picture of God is not of a benevolent grand-father sitting on a cloud tut-tutting when we go wrong. The Bible is full of calls for justice, for people to take full responsibility for their actions and being held to account for them. There is nothing un-Christian in that. Remember, however, that justice is not vengeance. Justice does not come by way of phone-ins, or slogans, or opinion polls on the Internet. Justice will not come by the rhetoric of politicians, or the inflaming of emotions, or the rekindling of old or new prejudices, but by careful, considered, impassionate weighing-up of evidence and with cooperation when applying the rule of law.

From the moment Adam and Eve exercised their choice in the garden, we have had the ability to choose, and it is one of the responsibilities of freedom that this can happen. However many debates we now have about the levels of security and how lax they were, we will never construct a society where this is impossible. This, I suspect, would be a society in which we would find it impossible to live.

I spoke for forty minutes on Thursday evening to our daughter in Washington, and I was asking her what the reaction was in the school. Remember it is a school which was very close to the Pentagon and with so many caught up with it in a real way. Despite all the emotion, and despite the desire for revenge, the debate in the school was for justice, not vengeance. One teacher, when addressing the school, said this: 'To descend to the level of terrorism and flatten Afghanistan will achieve nothing. We cannot descend to their level because we have been provoked and then the next day rise and return to being civilised. It is the price of freedom.' Yet they want justice, and so do we. There is no escaping the human dimension to this tragedy, and we must carefully consider the enormous importance of the political dimension to this tragedy.

Here in church, there is also a Christian dimension to this tragedy. Let me quote these words to you:

> In every untimely bereavement, whether in the quiet slipping from life of one most dearly loved, or whether it is the unlawful striking down of hundreds, our first act of pained, protesting faith is to turn to God in reproach. As Martha said, 'Lord, if you had been there, my brother, my sister, my beloved child would not have died'. Why did this happen to him or to her? Why was this disaster not averted by the touch of an almighty hand? Lord, if you had been there.

These are not my words but those of Professor James Whyte when he preached at the memorial service for the Lockerbie victims.

So, in some respect we have been here before, and we ask ourselves the same question: 'Where was God when all this happened?' Was he absent? Was he looking the other way? Was he somehow saying it is your world and you must thole it and get on with the results of your actions and your choices?

One of the reasons there are so many passages in the Bible that speak to us at this time is because the Bible is not a detached document escaping from the world, but was written by people who were pained by the world. The Christian faith is born out of pain and persecution, of suffering and loss. Therefore, Christian faith still speaks to us today. The Christian faith tells us that God was not absent, but there where we might least expect him:

- In the disaster
- In the tragedy
- In the suffering.

Because we see

- from Christmas to Easter
- from Bethlehem to Calvary
- to the Emmaus road.

That is the message of the Christian faith 'that God is not outside absent and untouched', but with us.

When Jesus hung upon the Cross, he might have reproached Martha who said 'Lord, if you had been here' and he was there, and, in that dying, set his seal upon our share of his suffering. So, when we cry to God in our pain, he understands.

5

We still ask ourselves why God did not prevent it. But, if we are going to ask ourselves that question, we must be consistent. If we wanted God's hand to reach out and prevent it, then God must also reach out and prevent us from gorging ourselves while one child dies in Africa every ten seconds from hunger. Do we really know what we say when we want God to intervene in our world? The God of the Bible and the Christ of the New Testament is not someone remote in judgement, but sharing in suffering. When the Apostle Paul speaks about God's comfort to those who are in trouble, it is because Christ suffered that he knows what we are doing.

It is not only pain and grief that we feel at this catastrophe, it is also anger. There is nothing wrong with that; and the Bible is also full of anger and indignation. It is not a sign of our weak faith that we feel angry and question if God is there. It is part of our living, growing faith. If you want any evidence of that, read the Book of Job. Job wanted to try to understand why he suffered, and he would not let go of his faith because that was too easy. Christ himself said: 'My God, why have you forsaken me?' If these words can find themselves on the lips of Christ, it does not diminish our faith if these words are on our lips as well.

There is nothing wrong with anger when faced with what we believe we are unable to face. There is nothing wrong with the desire for justice against those who perpetrated this evil. Yet we also know that God is with us in Christ, that in his suffering he shares our suffering, and he knows the pain we feel. He knows the feeling of the absence of God and the anger and the confusion that we have in our minds:

- He asks us not to suppress them;
- He asks us not to use them to diminish or lessen our faith;
- He asks us to bring them to him.

When he hung on that Cross, he knew the depths of human emotion and pain and suffering and loss. When we take it to him, we take it to someone who understands and who, in the fullness of time, will bind up our wounds.

I read recently of an incident in a concentration camp in Buchenwald in the Second World War. In one of the huts, there was a group of very learned Jews, many of whom were rabbis. One Sunday afternoon, in their despair, they decided that they would put God on trial because of their suffering. Witnesses came forward, some for the prosecution, some for the defence, and a bench of rabbis acted as the judge. In the light of their experiences, the case for the prosecution was overwhelming. Their community was being wiped out, most of their families had already been destroyed. 'How', as one said, 'could a good God permit this to happen?' The cases were put up, a desperate defence was made, but they had little difficulty in reaching their verdict. God was guilty as charged of neglecting his people. Silence fell upon the court, and then one elderly inmate rose to his feet. 'Nevertheless,' he said, 'it is time for our evening prayers.'

Amen.

NEWS NIGHT FRIDAY NIGHT? (handwritten)

Seasons

Sermon 2

Routine Revisited
(Transfiguration)

5 March 2003

Mark 9:2–9

It was the end of the service, and the minister was shaking hands with the congregation at the door. The little boy of one family was shaking the minister's hand warmly, and the minister was conscious that the little child was putting something in his hand. He looked down and saw a five-pence piece. 'Did you forget to put that in the collection?' 'No, that is for you. My dad has just said you are the poorest minister we have ever had.'

What we seek today on Transfiguration Sunday is an interpretation of this difficult passage that has something of that childlike quality of seeing the positive, and a way in which we can engage in it. The child was too young to be taken in by the cynicism and criticism of the world. The interpretation he made of his father's words was one that allowed him to engage in that interpretation, by giving something to the poorest minister that church had ever had.

If nothing else, I want us to try to explore something of that approach to this very different Transfiguration Sunday. I have heard and read many pieces on this passage that I am sure are theologically sound, linguistically clever and semantically very inventive. However, what does it say to us? Especially to those of us who feel so much more at home in the stories of Jesus helping and healing? We love the stories of Jesus criticising, or encouraging, or forgiving. Then, every now and again, one of these strange and unusual stories is thrown in as if to say 'Deal with this'. It is about mountain-tops and bleaching whiter than any powder we know, about clouds rolling in and voices from heaven.

Transfiguration Sunday – a special mountain-top experience, something that lifted the disciples from that which was everyday for them to something very special. That is not really a surprise to us in our own lives, because we all need lifting from the routine.

Perhaps for some of us, for you, it is the weekend. The week has been long and hard and we long for the weekend, we long for a break from the routine, to do those things that time and energy do not allow during the week, and we escape. Perhaps we play golf, visit family and friends, or we enjoy music, listening or playing. It is true of going on holiday, those special things that help us to recharge our batteries. However, in a sense, they are not a good parallel for our story because they do not bear much resemblance to what we are returning to. They may well give us more energy to return to the routine, but they are, in a sense, 'escapes' in their own right.

There are other special occasions which we celebrate which are breaks in themselves, but give us the opportunity to express something out of the routine. Remembering someone on their birthday, or anniversary, or that moment of promotion, or retirement, is all bound up in the routine but is a special moment that somehow takes it deeper and expresses something that we might not express at other times.

It is that model of something different and special that I think is more helpful to understand the Transfiguration. Something that lifts us out of the routine but also returns us to it as different people:

- more focused,
- more challenged,
- more renewed,
- more fresh,
- more forgiven,
- more loving,
- more loved,
- and not simply an escape in its own right.

For some of us, perhaps it is worship; for some of us, perhaps it is prayer; and, for some of us, it may well be the Sacrament of Holy Baptism today. For some, it may be the moment when couples come and commit themselves before God in marriage, an opportunity to express that which we might take for granted. However, the other side of that same coin is that it is only special because it does not happen all of the time. These mountain-top experiences, whatever they may be, are fleeting, and we must return to the everyday world.

Peter, that wonderfully attractive human, wants to stay there, he wants to share the glory – and, in Mark chapter 8, when Jesus predicts his suffering, Peter will have none of it. He says: 'You cannot suffer'. That denial of suffering prompts Jesus to say 'Get behind me, Satan'. Peter does not want the suffering, and he wants to build a memorial to the glory, but they cannot be separated. So, down the mountain they have to come, and Jesus heals a young boy. It is back to the ministry and back to the world with all its challenges, with its apathy and opposition. Yet, it is not back exactly as they were, for the disciples experienced Jesus in a way they had never experienced him before.

The description is interesting, but does not really take us very far in its own right, trying to describe the indescribable. Whatever they saw, whatever the experience

13

they had, it was a deep religious experience for them, and it reminded them that the man they followed was indeed the Son of God. It was a reminder of why they followed him, a reminder of the significance of that ministry and that sacrifice they would make, before they began that journey to Jerusalem. So, from that moment of setting Jesus apart at his baptism by saying 'You are my Son', the words of God now return to us. 'This is my Son, listen to him.'

So, they come down from the mountain, for they cannot stay there forever. They come with a renewed sense of who Jesus is, of whom they are following and of the ministry in which they are engaged. Later in the story, we will hear these things coming together, the mountain-top experience and the everyday routine to which we return. When the Son of Man comes in his glory, he will ask some to sit on his left, and some on his right. What will be the justification for that? 'When I was hungry, you gave me something to eat; when I was thirsty, you gave me something to drink.' Even in that most glorious special moment when the Son of Man returns, it will be linked to what we did in the everyday, away from the mountain-top. When we saw you hungry and thirsty, we fed you and gave you something to drink.

This special mountain-top moment gave the disciples and all who would see and hear it thereafter a glimpse of the glory of Christ. Perhaps they were at the stage that the words at Jesus' baptism were a distant memory. There had been all the ministry and the challenge in between, all the difficult teachings, all the opposition, all the tiredness, all the misunderstanding, so that those words at Jesus' baptism had become a distant memory. Here was a reminder of the glory of Christ, which was their motivation, their reason, their catalyst for being his people – and it happened on that mountain-top.

So, we should build no shelters, lest we try to remain on the high, and cut ourselves off from a world that is too hard, too cruel, too depressing with war looming. As Red Nose Day approaches, we shall see and hear all these images and pictures throughout our torn and fractured world.

How tempting it is, and how appealing, to follow in Peter's footsteps, lifted and separated from the world. What a glorious moment it is to glimpse the glory of Christ! Let us build shelters and remain here. No! Down the mountain we must come, back to the routine and back to the unexpected which lies before us:

- perhaps we will not be the same?
- perhaps there will be something in our worship today?
- perhaps something you will have read, or said, or prayed?
- perhaps there will be something in the Sacrament of Holy Baptism or in the Sacrament of Holy Communion?

Something that will for a moment give you that mountain-top experience: that glimpse of the glory of Christ. All of this is intended to remind us why we are here and whom it is we follow. Then we will indeed return from the mountain-top. We will return to this week with all that it brings, known and unknown, but perhaps not quite the same as we were when we arrived.

'This is my beloved Son, listen to him'.

Amen.

Where Might We Find Healing?
(Passion Sunday)

1 April 2001

Luke 23:1–25

On Passion Sunday, we remember specifically the suffering and the death of our Lord Jesus Christ, the central theme of the Cross. Some years ago, *Time Magazine* carried out a survey among 100 of the most prominent American citizens. They gave them a list of 100 important events and asked them to place them in order of importance with regard to their significance to the world. When the survey was published, it made interesting reading.

Perhaps you will not be surprised to know that first place was given to Christopher Columbus, who discovered America. Three events shared fourteenth place – the discovery of X-rays, the Wright brothers' first flight and the Crucifixion of Jesus Christ. When those who conducted the survey realised what had happened they went back to the 100, realising that ninety-seven of them were professing Christians, yet the Cross appeared as fourteenth equal in importance. They replied that this was a secular survey; it was not done by the Church. If the Church had asked us, we would have put it first!

While to some that might be mildly amusing, there is a real paradox behind this. That which we can easily affirm in the atmosphere of worship we find difficult to affirm outside. I suspect not many of you will be talking about the Cross tomorrow morning at your work. Here, in the atmosphere of worship, we will happily sing and pray about the glories and the power of the Cross. 'In the Cross of Christ I glory'; 'Lift high the Cross'; 'When I survey the wondrous Cross'.

The German philosopher and poet, Goethe, wrote: 'I hate four things above everything else: tobacco smoke, lice, garlic, and the Cross'. Perhaps in some ways it is understandable. We, as a generation, are more sensitive to the issue of death than many previous ones. Because people live longer, and science and medicine have advanced so much, you can no longer say someone has had a good innings unless they are well past 85. Therefore, we do not like the subject of the Cross, because it speaks about death, and it is not a subject we are comfortable with.

In terms of the Christian Church, we would rather go straight to the Easter bunnies. It is a lovely story. It concerns new life and Easter eggs and the empty tomb. Life is hard enough between Monday and Saturday; Sunday should be a time of escapism, of encouragement, of renewal. Do not talk about death, it depresses me and I do not come to church to be depressed. Is it any surprise then that many, particularly in the Protestant tradition, shy away from the Cross? I have lost count of the number of Protestant Reformed Churches I have been in and have not seen a Cross anywhere in the building.

If we think about it, there are, as Hans Küng once said, many who hang on the Cross. Those who are worn out by burdens of care and worry, the oppressed and discriminated against, those who are overwhelmed by the demands placed upon them, the bored, those who are crushed by fear, those whose hearts are poisoned by hate, who believe they have been forgotten by their friends and feel themselves to be ignored by the world. In some sense, is it not true that everyone is hanging on his or her own particular cross? (See Hans Küng, *The Church*, Burns & Oates, 1969.)

If we scratch the surface of the façade that we are up to the job that is entrusted to us, that we are not always broken, that our faith is strong, underneath there will be trials and tribulations, fears, anxieties and temptations, affecting everyone, of which we have no idea. They are crosses nonetheless. Sometimes these crosses have come about through circumstances, illness, bereavement, lone- liness, redundancy, family break-ups and family tensions. Perhaps they are crosses that our personalities force on us simply by the kind of people we are:

- Bitter people who will never forget and who will carry that cross all their lives.
- Anxious people who are anxious, even if there is nothing to be anxious about.
- Spiteful people who only know the hollow victory of some petty triumph which they enjoy endlessly.
- Even sensitive people who know that to survive in this world you need to grow a thicker skin, but do not know how to do it.

Perhaps the cross we bear is because of the conditions in which we live and, if not us, then others in the world. Poverty, oppression, injustice, our personalities, our experiences, can all be the crosses on which we hang. Küng was right when he said: 'Is not everyone hanging on his or her own Cross?'

Now, it might be a valid thing to say that this is to trivialise the cross of Christ, the central point of our Christian faith, and to drag in all the neuroses and the anxieties and the problems that we have and somehow to elevate them to the Cross of Christ. However, it was Christ himself who said: 'Take up your cross and follow me'. He did not say: 'Take up my Cross and follow me'. He asked us to take up that cross on which we hang, whatever it is, and to follow him – and that is one movement, not two. Is not everyone hanging on his or her own cross?

In other words, it is not to trivialise what Jesus went through to compare it with our own experience, but to try to make sense of the Cross, in the light of our experience. We do not like doing that because to bear a cross, and to recognise that we are carrying it, is somehow in this modern world a sign of defeat, a sign of not being able to cope, a sign of being vulnerable. None of these things is good news in the world in which we live and work. Indeed, admitting to any of these could seriously damage your promotion prospects.

Jesus said: 'Take up *your* cross and follow me'. It is an unreasonable question to ask: 'Where are you going?' We are following Jesus to his Cross, and we are taking our crosses with us – and it is there, at Golgotha, that all crosses meet. 'Take up your cross and follow me all the way to Calvary.'

What happens when we take our crosses there? Lonely people will discover in Christ on the Cross a loneliness that they could not ever imagine or experience.

Bitter people who have a grudge that they will not let go will discover at the Cross of Christ a reason for bitterness that they could never even understand.

People who are broken in their health, in their mind, will discover brokenness at the Cross that they could not begin to imagine.

If that is the case, why take it there? Why go to a psychiatrist who is more depressed than you are? Why ask someone for money who has less money that you have?

Why take your cross, depressing as it might be, to that ultimate Cross of all – Calvary. *It is because we know that that experience does not finish there* – that the lonely who take that cross of loneliness to the Cross of Christ and see him in all his loneliness also see and hear him say: 'Father, into your hands I commit my spirit'. Embittered people who will not forgive and forget, who find at the Cross a reason for being bitter, will also hear him say: 'Father, forgive them'. Those who are broken in mind and in body, and simply see a reflection of their own experience at the Cross, will also see and hear the resurrected Christ promising that we will be with him in paradise. It is not for a mutual depressing session that we take our crosses to Calvary, but to see them resolved and to experience for ourselves why Christ came and why he died. Jesus invites us to take our cross to Calvary because there we will meet God. In all its vulnerability, in all its risks, in all its pain, we will see it triumph, because that is why the Cross is at the centre of the Christian faith.

That is why we do not jump from the beginning of Lent to the joys of Easter, but we take and experience the journey of Lent and Passion Sunday to remind ourselves of the full significance of the Cross, to hear again the full injunction from him to follow him with our own cross, to go on a journey to be where it is resolved, and, in so doing, to take the risk of being vulnerable, the possibility of being rejected, the possibility of others seeing how vulnerable we are.

Bernard Levin once interviewed the playwright Dennis Potter at the time of his very controversial play *The Son of Man*. In the discussions about the faith, Potter finished with one memorable phrase. In the discussions about the Christian faith the playwright suggested that, while many who are suffering in the world believe that Christianity operates like a bandage, he did not. Instead, he indicated that he believed that Christianity should be perceived not as a bandage but as a wound. Pick up your cross and follow me. Follow me all the way to Calvary, that place where all our crosses meet and where all will find peace and healing within.

Amen.

Community, Communication and Courage
(Pentecost)

4 June 2006

Acts 2:1–21

T oday is the day of Pentecost. We read the words, but we find it hard to understand. The words are before us, but what do they mean?

Three days into our holiday, sitting in Nairobi in Kenya, we received a telephone call from our daughter to tell us that our manse had been broken into. Jennifer was in the house at the time, asleep in bed, and she noticed the front door open in the morning. The laptop computers had gone, the flat-screen television had gone; those who know me know just exactly what that means. Jennifer's bag was taken, and a few days later the police phoned to say that the bag had been recovered. 'The passport has gone, your glasses have gone, your i-Pod has gone, but your bank cards are there and your money is there.' 'My money is there?' 'Yes, your money is here', said the policeman. 'How much did you have?' She said 'Two £20 notes'. 'They've left the Scottish one.' They looked at a Clydesdale Bank £20 note and they read it and they still could not understand it. Every cloud ...

So, just what do we do with the day of Pentecost?

- We are much happier with Christmas.
- It is a lovely time.
- It is identifiable.

• It has echoes of our childhood and is full of so many activities within our family life.

Sometimes, we are happier even with the more miraculous events of Easter. However, any notion, any talk, any definition of the Holy Spirit leaves many good, blue-blooded Presbyterians a bit cold. We know what the Spirit means to some, the way it manifests itself. We will just stick to Christmas and Easter, because they are much safer. The more the Church has tried to create a theology of Pentecost, sometimes the more confusing it is, because what happened first was the experience of the people of God. The theology came out of the experience, and not the other way around.

So, when we read the events of Pentecost, what can we take out of it for now, even allowing for the fact that some wanted to hi-jack the Holy Spirit for their own purpose and their own definition? One writer put it this way: 'There have always been groups in the Church who manipulate the Holy Spirit and consider it their own property. Even in the earliest days, the Church fell prey to false enthusiasm, and some claimed that the Holy Spirit was especially at work in them'.

This is still true in many parts of the Church in our world. On the other hand, there are churches from whom the spirit – the spirit of life, the spirit of energy, the spirit of change, the spirit of passion and warmth – seems to have departed. Churches may be cramped in wintry formalisms and petrified structures. The test of the presence of the Holy Spirit is whether the life and the love of Jesus Christ, as we see it in the gospels, is reflected in us. To use an old biblical phrase, 'The Spirit takes the things of Christ and makes them ours'.

I

Acts chapter 2, verses 1–21 are familiar words. What do they say to us now about the spirit of Pentecost? I think the first thing is that Pentecost is about *community*. At the beginning of chapter 2, the disciples were all together in one place. This fulfils the promise that the Spirit would come, but it was not a promise to individual Christians. When they were all together in one place as the community of the early Church, the Spirit came upon them. As a result, each of them testified as the Spirit gave them power. Each of them testified. The Spirit works in each of us in different ways. We have different gifts to offer, we have different talents to bring to the life of the Church. The place where we exercise and share that is in the community of faith, where we receive not only that Spirit but also the encouragement of all those around us. Those who wish to hi-jack the Spirit for a particular group within the Church or individuals cannot base that on Acts chapter 2 verse 1. When they were together in one place, they experienced the Spirit.

II

The second thing I want to say about Pentecost is that, while it also speaks about community, it speaks about *communication*. The great thing about Pentecost is that people were hearing the great things of God in their own tongue, and hearing is quite different from listening.

On 25 May, when we were in Cape Town, our hotel had Internet access. I thought it would be fun to listen in to our General Assembly, which was being broadcast live on the Internet. Their equipment was very sophisticated, and I got in without any bother and saw that very familiar view of the Assembly, with some familiar faces – but I suddenly realised that the computer system had no speakers, so I could not hear a word. Some of you might think that was amusing, and perhaps I was seeing the Assembly at its best. However, I had no papers with me, and I had no idea what they were saying. Some who went to the Assembly said:

'We heard every word and we still do not know what they were saying'. My father used to say to me: 'I know you are listening, but are you hearing?'

In other words, we are not saying we *heard* the disciples, we are saying we heard the disciples speak of the great things that God has done. There is an understanding, there is an empathy that comes from us, sharing the Word of God in the Spirit. How often do people listen to the Church, genuinely seeking some purpose and some meaning in their life? By what we say and what we do, can they really hear us? Or rather, not *us* but the great things that God can still do in and through his people in the power of the Spirit. How is it that we can hear in our own tongue?

Think of the very private ways in which God and Christ revealed themselves to the wise men and a few shepherds at Christmas, to a few disciples in the upper room, to the disciples on top of the mountain of ascension, but not any more. Now the Spirit speaks through his people. This is an awesome responsibility. In the things we say and do as individuals and the Church, people will hear and see the great things that God is doing.

Pentecost is about community; they were all together in one place. Pentecost is about communication; they could hear what great things God is still doing because of the testimony of his people.

III

Pentecost is also about *courage*. Peter stood up before them, the same Peter who time and time again missed the point when he was with Jesus, the same Peter who denied Jesus at the time of his Crucifixion, that same Peter now with the courage to stand up and speak.

The day on which I had been slightly disappointed by my silent Assembly was 25 May, Ascension Day. So, in the evening, Hilda and I went to St George's Cathedral in Cape Town, the former seat of Archbishop Desmond Tutu. I was fascinated with the preacher, who was black. What he said in his sermon was this: 'Apartheid may have gone as a legal system, but has life changed for most black people? If you go to the townships, would you notice any difference? If you asked 80 per cent of the population of South Africa if their life was any different, what would they say?' Seventy per cent of the congregation was white, and it was quite clear from the reaction of the congregation during and after, that those who were white fully supported what that black preacher was saying.

In many ways, the Church is still at the cutting edge of reaching those on the margins. All around that church, throughout the bookstall, on the posters, in the seminars and the discussions, there was one topic and one topic only; it was in that church from top to bottom. It was HIV and AIDS.

Pentecost is about community and communication, but also the courage to tackle the issues that are real for the people of God. We have to tackle the issues that are real for us in twenty-first-century London in the same way as those in St George's Cathedral in Cape Town are tackling the issues real for the people whom they are called to serve. Pentecost is also about the courage to stand up and speak.

In our passage from Acts, the disciples were expecting the end of the world. They were quoting from the poet Joel. 'And all the wonderful things we will see as the end is approaching.' Now the churches have to cope with the fact that the end was not then. Who knows when it will be?

- For some, it might still be the end of oppression, if we have the courage to speak in the Spirit.
- For some, it might be the end of hunger, if we have the courage to speak in the Spirit.

- For some, it might be the end of prejudice and misunderstanding, if we have the courage to speak in the Spirit.

I was not at the Assembly, obviously, and I did not hear it. I wish I had been there, for no other debate than the debate on civil partnerships. Not because I wanted to take part in the debate, but because I wanted to say to the Assembly: 'We should not be debating this'. Ministers and the people of God must be able to be moved by the Spirit to respond pastorally to those in their midst. You will never codify this in law. The Spirit blows where it will. The more often we try legislation, the clumsier and the more awkward and vindictive we become. The minute we want to have legislation, we have some who will vote for it and some who will vote against it.

We should not be debating this. Not because we are ducking issues, but because we need to leave room for the power of the Spirit to move us, as the people of God. We are here to share the love and the compassion of God as we see the Spirit move us and not with a reference to a page and a sub-section. Those of you who know me well would know how I would have voted anyway. The result is not the problem. The debate is. The power of the Spirit came upon the Church and can still come upon the Church.

I hope and pray that we, as the people of God here in this place, may be a community, may be ready to communicate with one another, with the world outside, as God communicates with us, will have the courage to let the Spirit of God flow in us. So, then, what people might see is the love and the compassion of Christ poured out for his people.

Amen.

Where Might Jesus Be Seen?
(Christ the King)

24 November 2002

Matthew 25:31–46

> If we had only known, we would have acted differently.
> When did we see you hungry and gave you nothing to eat?
> When did we see you thirsty and gave you nothing to
> drink? When did we see you naked and did not clothe you?
> If we had only known.

Last night, there was a fascinating programme on BBC2 about Windsor Castle. It was interesting because it traced the development of the castle and, in so doing, showed us the change and the development in the monarchy. It began with the castle in its original form, with crude structures perched on a hill whose only function really was defence – to defend the people, to invite the people under your rule into the stronghold of the castle and to keep the invaders away.

Then, of course, we saw the castle change as the monarchy developed; it became more formalised, more structured. The person who was originally showing evidence of courage and vision and leadership was elected to the position of king. Gradually, it became a more formal role, creating and administering laws and justice. It became a much more elevated position, an institution in its own right. The people moved outside the castle walls, for the king needed it all to himself.

There were two fascinating periods in the programme: the period around the time of Charles II, and then the time around George III and IV. This was the time when the most money was spent on Windsor Castle, when the institution of the monarchy was at its height, when the money spent on art, furniture and silver knew no bounds. The whole idea of being at court, about correct pecking order, about who could see the king and the queen and who could not, happened at the time the power of the monarchy was at its lowest. Parliament ruled, and the monarch tried to compensate.

What place for Christ the King?

Now we move to a time when things are a little more democratic and the castle gates are open, even for a price. People are now encouraged to come in, by a monarchy which I think is still struggling to find its role in the twenty-first century.

Could that in any way be a parallel of the Church? Can we see the Church beginning as simply a stronghold, either physical or spiritually, with the leadership, the courage, the sacrifice, the compassion of its leader, Christ, who drew people to him? Can we see the development of an institution where there is no longer sanctuary in the church, but the people live outside? Can we see the development of the institution of the Church in its lavishness, its rules and regulations, at a time when its power was at its least? Is it now opening its doors, but still struggling to find its relevance in the twenty-first century? So what place then for Christ the King?

Our reading from Matthew's gospel really has to be taken in context, for it comes at the end of a series of parables which were all trying to divine what the end of an age would be. No-one knows when the Son of Man is going to come back – so we had better be ready. In the earlier chapters of Matthew's gospel, we have the readings about coming like a thief in the night, when no-one will know or be prepared. Then we have five foolish virgins, and the five wise virgins who had their lamps filled with oil and the wicks trimmed ready. Then, just in case we got the impression that, while waiting for Christ to return, we simply wait with our lamps on our lap, we have the parable of the talents. Waiting, yes – but we must be active, we must invest that which Christ has given us, and invest it in the world, and produce a harvest while we are waiting.

The whole series will come to an end with the return of the Son of Man. The king shall sit on this throne and he will judge. How prepared will you be, and how active have you been with the talents given to you? Then we go into what must have been one of the most familiar stories, of the sheep and the goats. When did we see you hungry and thirsty and naked? When did we give you something to eat, something to drink, when did we see it was you? Surely then the injunction is quite clear.

What a shock it might be if we do get to the pearly gates and we are asked to account for our lives. We are standing, trembling!

- Will it be that tube fare that I avoided?
- That little bit I omitted to put into my tax return?
- The lawnmower I held on to for too long?
- The telephone call I never made?
- The reply I never wrote?
- Some of the words I said in great haste that I know caused some hurt?
- Some of the words that needed to be spoken by me at a time when I remained silent?

How we could be standing fidgeting, wondering what the king on his throne will say to us as we take account of our life, and it is none of these things? It is none of these things because they are all part of us being obsessed by ourselves. He will say to the righteous: 'Come and receive your inheritance, for when I was hungry you gave me something to eat, when I was thirsty you gave me something to drink'. They will be astonished and unable to recall when they did it.

Is that a reminder that God's purposes will not be thwarted? Those who might receive the eternal blessing might be those who are not in the Church at all. Might it be that the designation of 'righteous' will be because of what they did, not because of who they thought they were? Moreover, they were not even aware of it.

If we had only known that that is what Jesus meant – *but we do know.* We do know, in this dramatic picture in Matthew, that when the king comes to judge, it will be how we reacted to those in the margins. This is not rocket science. It is stating what are the very basics of life – food and water, and health and freedom – and it is engaging in these things that seem to be the things of the kingdom. We know the story; we cannot say to Jesus any more, if we ever could, if we had only known what he meant. *We know what he meant.* It seems a world apart. How many of us know someone who is really thirsty and hungry? How many of us know someone who is in prison? How hard it is for us to close that gap between the gospel we cherish and the world in which we live!

Financial generosity is only the beginning

We know whom to help – and we do. This congregation is among the most generous I have ever come across in trying to tackle these things through some of the projects which will be well known to you – our Lenten project, our Napier Fund, our appeals, our retiring collections, all of which are wonderfully supported by you. However, I think that this parable is telling us that that is only the beginning and not an end in itself.

The key comes towards the end of that phrase of saying these familiar passages about when you were hungry or thirsty, or in prison, sick and naked. What Jesus did *not* say was: 'Every time you do anything to the least of my brothers, you clock up brownie points'. He said: 'It is as if you are doing it to me'.

Now suddenly the picture changes. If somehow our relationship changes with the world, and those on the margins mirror our relationship with Christ, then we become involved, we invest something of ourselves, we open ourselves to compassion and love and to being hurt. It is about relationships, it is about sacrifice, it is about giving that which will cost us the most, for we would not dream of giving Christ anything that was, in a sense, a token and which ultimately cost us little. Everything you do for the least of my brothers, it is as if you are doing it for me. This lies at the very core of our faith. What a challenge for those of us who in our daily life come across very few people who are thirsty and hungry, in prison, or homeless!

Who is my neighbour?

Last Sunday night, we had Lord Hope sharing with us something of his faith and something of the law and the Church. He quoted a famous story, well known to many and especially in Scotland, the subject of many children's addresses, including one from me. It is the famous case in Paisley, just outside Glasgow, of the bottle of ginger beer. A lady bought a bottle of ginger beer in a café. Ginger-beer bottles were, and still are, opaque – you cannot see through them. When she poured out the ginger beer, out popped a decomposed slug. Naturally, she was upset. She wanted to sue the manufacturer of the ginger beer. Up until then, you could only sue someone with whom you had a contract – and the contract was with the café-owner who had sold her the bottle.

However, as the legal case developed, Lord Atkins gave his famous Atkins dictum, and he quoted Scripture: 'Who is my neighbour? Anyone affected by my actions.' This landmark case changed the face of European law because of the slug in the bottle. Suddenly, my neighbour is not just the person next door, or the person sitting in front, but anyone who might be affected by my actions.

What a traumatic thought that is, and how it opens up the world! Anyone affected by my actions could mean individually and collectively:

- as a church
- as a nation
- as a government
- as a European Union.

No longer is a neighbour defined as someone with whom we have eye contact in the world in which we live. So there is a global sense in which we say: 'Every time you do anything for the least of my brethren, you do it for me'. It is:

- a question of understanding
- of reaching out
- of compassion and tolerance
- about the courage to refuse to sustain the systems that make people thirsty and hungry and lonely and abused
- the attitudes that make people going to prison – the vast bulk of whose crimes would not keep us awake at night – feel totally neglected by society as second-class citizens.

We need to remind ourselves that that old cliché is true, that Christ was not crucified in a cathedral between two candles, but on a hill between two thieves. If we had only known – *but we do know* and, as we said last Sunday, we are called to use the talents, the resources, the gifts that God has given us, to invest them in the world in which we are set, to produce a return for his kingdom, that we might help to shape our society. To shape a world where those who are hungry will be fed, those who are thirsty are given something to drink, those who are in prison (and at this time of the year we remember them particularly), while they may very well be serving the due punishment for their crimes, are not made to feel less than human, or debarred from knowing the peace of Christ.

Someone famously once said that interviewing a well-known politician was like being savaged by a dead sheep. I know we are not dead sheep – but, because of all the calls on our time and our money, how often we are goats in sheep's clothing. So we will not achieve these ends by our own merits, but by the grace of God working in and through us. When we see the hungry and the thirsty, and the homeless and those in prison and those in hospital, our eyes must be opened to see Christ in them, as well as they should be able to in us.

Amen.

Sayings of Jesus

Commitment, Collective Action and Conformity

25 April 2004

John 21:1–19

The former Moderator of the General Assembly of our Church, the Very Rev. Andrew McLellan, referring to the frequency with which the Moderator is called on to address gatherings, said that, to him, the most daunting challenge usually came at the end. 'Moderator, would you say a few words before you go?' How do you leave people with an appropriate word in keeping with everything you have been trying to do? When I left my previous parish in Stirling, what I said on my last Sunday was the hardest thing I had to say.

Today, our reading is taken from the last chapter of John's gospel. Most commentators agree that John's gospel finishes at verse 19, and that what follows was added by the early Church to deal with some very real and pressing issues. The academics are fairly at one in saying that the gospel finishes at verse 19. So, it is to the end of verse 19 that we look for the final word. Not final, of course, in the sense that the word is relevant and forever with us, but the last one from Jesus' own lips. After all that Jesus has said, done and achieved, how will he round off his life on earth? How will he round off his ministry? What will he say by way of culmination of all that he has gone through? What will be the final word?

Perhaps we should start with a few brief words of explanation and setting for our reading, more by way of saying what we are *not* going to deal with. We know the significance of Jesus asking Peter three times 'Do you love me?' and so securing his forgiveness for denying him three times. We see the significance when the disciples have gone back to work, when, whatever the tragedy, whatever the disappointment, or even the excitement, life still goes on, they need to make a living, so they are back fishing. The significance of Jesus feeding them with loaves and fishes implies that we are back to the feeding of the 5,000, with all the overtones of communion.

The final word – what is it? Jesus says 'Follow me', which is how he sums up his ministry. In other words, it does not end here. What happens now, lest all that has gone before has been in vain, rests with you. Follow me. The injunction to follow comes after he puts a question, and a challenge, to Peter. Only in the light of Peter's response does he challenge him to follow him. 'Peter, do you love me?' 'Then feed my sheep.'

You will not be surprised to know that I want to say three things about that this morning. The first is a call to *commitment*, the second is a call to *collective action*, and the third is a call to *conform*.

Commitment

Firstly, it is a call to commitment. The dictionary defines commitment as an obligation undertaken, an attachment to a doctrine or a cause. Commitment is not a very common word in our time! We find it very hard to get people to commit themselves to anything. We live in a 'pick and mix' society. People want to have lots of experiences, but will, or do, not commit themselves to any one in particular. Anyone in this day and age who requires people to sign up to a commitment sees their numbers dwindling. The church, uniformed organisations for our young people and political parties are, at the moment, showing their lowest membership since any of these organisations began.

We live in a time when people do not want to join anything. Commitment is something we sometimes longingly look back at. In the good old days, people would become elders for forty years and Sunday School teachers for fifty – God bless them! Now we cannot get people to do anything – and, if they do, it is for a year, or two, or three at the most, because all our lives are busy. We cannot possibly commit ourselves to longer than that.

However, we return again to the circumstances in which Jesus posed a challenge. He only posed it because Peter said 'Yes' to the question. We are not stopping people on the street and asking them why they are not committed to the church, but only those who have already said 'Yes' to the question 'Do you love me?' In other words, we are asking those who have already confessed their commitment with their lips: can they support it with their lives? It was only when Peter said 'Yes' to that question that Jesus said 'Feed my sheep and follow me'.

It is a call for commitment; but, having said that, we as a church must be careful that we do not organise ourselves with an ongoing mid-nineteenth-century model of the church and its witness and then wonder why people cannot commit themselves because life is different. Eleven o'clock in the morning, when we worship, was a time to accommodate milking in the rural communities of the nineteenth century.

So, when we call for commitment, we must organise ourselves in such a way that people can commit themselves – because, if they are not committing to our model, we then make a very rash assumption that they are not committed. I do not believe that to be the case. I believe there is a lot of commitment, especially among our young people, flying around, looking for a cause. We must try to give people the opportunity to express and develop that commitment as part of their discipleship.

That is why we are introducing our midweek service which begins this Wednesday and will run every Wednesday between 1 and 1:20pm. It is a genuine attempt to give people another opportunity to come and worship, albeit in a slightly different style. We live in a world where Sundays have difficulties that were not there 100 years ago and the church must respond to them. Soon you will see an intimation for our experimental early services for the month of August at 9:30am, specifically designed for children and young families to worship together. There will be no Summer Sunday Club in the hall, because we all need a break from the hall, especially our children. We ask ourselves: when was the last time any of the children in this church heard a benediction? They must learn to worship together. It is an opportunity; we hope to widen the chance for people to make their commitment.

Collective action

The second thing I would suggest is that it is a call to *collective action*. Commitment is not just about people turning up to church. We are not so possessive and closed-minded as to think that the only gauge of commitment is the numbers in the pews. Jesus said to Peter: 'Feed my sheep'. Now, nominally, sheep feed themselves with a little encouragement at certain times of the year; but this was a clear injunction for Peter and the disciples and for Christian generations thereafter to feed the sheep who cannot feed themselves – those who need help.

'Do you love me? Then feed my sheep.' There is no separating them; there is no having one without the other.

'Help those who need help, for that is the way you express your love for me', said Jesus. It gives me the opportunity to say a very sincere thank you to everyone who contributed over £10,000 to our Lenten Appeal for the orphanage in Romania. I'm going to ask you again – this time, it is Christian Aid. We need your help. We need your time and we need your resources. These are not optional extras; it is the crux of the faith. It is not something we engage in if we have money left over and we have time to spare. It is the essence of the gospel. Jesus said: 'Do you love me? Then feed my sheep.'

When Jesus asked 'do you love me?' and Peter said 'yes', Jesus did not reply: 'well, that is nice to know'. 'Feed my sheep' is the way we express that love for Christ. It is not possible for us as Christians to become compassion-weary. It is not an option. We must try to make sure that that call to commitment and collective action is made meaningful and manageable. People know where their money is going; people feel that there is an ownership in the project. They believe that it is being used in a worthwhile way, that the money will not be abused. They are not excuses for not feeding the sheep simply because it is too difficult.

So when, during the intimations, I give Christian Aid the hard sell, please, please do not say 'not more appeals for money!' If you can answer that question from Jesus, and he is putting it to us again as we gather at his table, 'Do you love me?', if the answer is 'Yes', you know what for. It is direct to all of us: 'Feed my sheep', said Jesus. Then something of worth and beauty might emerge at times of despair and suffering.

Conformity

The final word is this. It is a call to conform. Now, that is not a popular one. If I had encouraged some of you to invite your children to worship because the minister was going to speak about the need to conform, if they came, it would be to disagree. By conform, I mean us to conform ourselves to the mind of Christ, not to the traditions of the Church. Meaningful as they are, but liable to change, it is not to conform to any statutes, or creeds, which become increasingly irrelevant to young people and their lives. It is to conform, to become the same as, to obey Christ himself. In Romans, Paul says to anyone who would read and listen: 'Let your mind be transformed after the mind of Christ'.

There is a big challenge in there, because we remind ourselves that Jesus said 'Feed *my* sheep'. He did not say 'Feed your sheep'. It is not for us to choose, but for Christ to choose for us – and that is painful. Some people might say: 'The orphanage for the children is very appealing. Christian Aid is a bit dodgy. It is too political. It has supported things in the past I am not too sure about.'

Jesus said: 'Feed *my* sheep, not yours' – and, if you look back through his ministry, we need to be honest and say he chose people who were diseased, and the significance of that, of course, is that people felt that the disease was the victim's own fault. Do we feel the same about AIDS? He associated with prostitutes, quislings of the day who supported a corrupt government of the day against their own people. Let us not be too quick to say 'What a wonderful idea' unless we realise that Jesus said: 'Feed *my* sheep – the ones I have chosen, the ones I have identified as needing my gospel and my help'. Sometimes that need might be non-material, but the need might still be great.

Let us then gather around his table to be nourished and fed, for that is the only way we will be able to attempt to respond in the way we should. He asks us the same question today as he asked Peter: 'Do you love me?' Let us be nourished at this table before we are too quick to answer 'Yes, Lord, you know that I love you,' – because, when we say that, he will say to us as he says to every generation: 'Then feed my sheep and follow me'.

Amen.

Lost in Translation: The Yoke of Jesus

3 July 2005

Matthew 11:16–19, 25–30

London was quite a place to be yesterday. In descending order of importance:

- our senior citizens' outing yesterday
- a wedding here in the church
- Live 8 in Hyde Park
- The Gay and Lesbian Pride March in Battersea
- The Wimbledon Ladies' final, and
- The NatWest final at Lords.

So, plenty to choose from. I suppose, if there was anything that connected them, it is the concept of commitment. We see evidence of commitment to the sport, or commitment to the cause, or commitment to the welfare of others. For various reasons, it was a day when commitment was high on the agenda in London.

Our son, Philip, was a steward yesterday at the march in Edinburgh when a quarter of a million people marched. He was saved the sight of ageing pop stars who have made their millions but lost their voices and who irritated me by taking a moral high ground and lecturing us on the problems of Africa. That was not the power of Live 8, it was the sheer weight of humanity's protest.

So, that was all very powerful yesterday – and then I kept returning to our reading today from Matthew's gospel and that beautiful quotation. Is there a lovelier quotation in Scripture? Sadly, we often only use it at funerals. 'Come to me all who are weary and whose load is heavy, and I will give you rest. Take my yoke upon you and learn from me, for I am gentle and humble-hearted and you will find rest for your soul.' Is that the message that the Church has to offer? This message is

- very moving
- very beautiful
- very powerful in settings like funerals.

Yet, what is it saying about 'Make Poverty History?'

- What is it saying about the abuse of human rights in Zimbabwe and Burma and in so many other places?
- Has the danger been that the Church loses its voice, and its only redress is saying to people: 'Come to me you whose load is heavy, and I will give you rest'?

When I was reading some commentaries on this part of Matthew, one or two writers pointed out the problem that it is a very radical and powerful passage which is very difficult to translate. It is not just a semantic problem, but it loses some of its power by the words we use. When I read this, I suddenly realised that it says much more to us as the leaders prepare to meet at the G8 summit at Gleneagles. 'Come to me all who are weary and whose load is heavy' – so far so good. Surely that refers not just to most, if not all of us in our lives, but especially to the leaders of the G8 nations? It is easy to criticise politicians; and some deserve it, but others are deeply moved by the plight of others. They are desperate to do something about the problems of the world, and there is no easy solution. Those who meet at Gleneagles bear a heavy load, and their task is great. Jesus said: 'Come to me all whose load is heavy, burdened by the responsibilities they carry'.

The problem with our translation of the rest of it is that it seems like it is some kind of emotional or spiritual rest, a kind of contemplation. Just come and sit and be quiet and relax and note the peace of God. However, what will that do with poverty in Africa? The original is really more powerful. 'Take my yoke upon you', says Jesus. The concerns that I have, the priorities that I have been following. This is the yoke you should carry. So Jesus said: 'My yoke is easy'. Now, that's a bad translation. A better translation is not 'easy'; the word is 'appropriate'. If we use that word, then it is quite different. In other words, perhaps Jesus is saying: 'I will not ask you to carry anything that is indeed too much of a burden for you. What you are being asked to carry is within your power, it is within your abilities to do something about it. Take my yoke upon you and learn from me, for it is appropriate for you.'

So, for the G8 leaders, what is appropriate for them is to use the astonishing power and authority that they have. What is appropriate for us is to use the resources and the talent that we have, to take upon ourselves not the yoke of our own choosing, or our own making, not the priorities and the prejudice that seem to occupy so much of our lives, but the yoke of promise. Jesus' concern is expressed for the poor, the children and the marginalised. It is also present for the wealthy, as well as the poor and the burdens that they all carry. 'Come to me all who are weary and are heavily laden.' We all carry burdens.

Everyone's heart today carries a burden of some kind, perhaps completely unknown to those who sit around us – sometimes even unknown to those with whom we live, and the yoke is heavy. The leaders of the nations carry a yoke of responsibility and authority and power, and what Zechariah reminds us of today is just exactly what this Christian power is – a King will come, and he will ride in humility on a donkey. There is, in a sense, the balance; there is the challenge to have power and humility that sit together as we see them in Christ.

It is very powerful to see all these people moved onto the streets. Peaceful protest is very powerful, and I am quite sure that the leaders of the G8 nations have heard it, and it will not make their challenge any easier. The complex relationships, the complex politics, economics, sociology and religions of our world do not make it easy. One thing we do remember, as one of our past Moderators said this week, is that 'Poverty is a social construct. It is there because we allow it to be there and we could remove it.'

We are in enough anguish at natural disaster. When the tsunami came, there was a feeling of helplessness. When disease seems to strike those who seem to deserve it least, we seem helpless; but poverty is not the same. Poverty is a social construct which, in our shame, we allow to continue. One of the most moving parts of the concert was when the ageing pop star moved aside and the African Children's Choir appeared. This is the same choir who will present a concert in this very church in July. At the last minute, they were invited. It was just a brief reminder of the reality amid all these horrendous pictures which often give us compassion fatigue. Suddenly, there were these African children who were bright, who were smiling, who were singing in tune. 'Do not pity us, but help us. Give us our dignity and our self-respect. Construct a world where poverty will be history.' Jesus finishes that wonderful phrase by saying: 'If you come to me, if you take my yoke upon you – my yoke, my concerns, my priorities, that which drives my ministry – then you will find rest'.

I have been to so many funerals where ministers finish on that: 'Come to me and I will give you rest'. But that is not how the passage finishes. There is a hymn that says that; there is a chant that says that: 'Come to me and I will give you rest'. However, the result of that challenging yoke of Christ is not rest in the sense of an absence of activity. What Scripture says is that we will find rest for your souls. In other words, there will be a fulfilment to that deep longing, that deep spirituality, that wants to do something about the problems of the world. You find rest for your souls. My yoke will touch parts that other causes will not reach. That is the challenge of the Christian gospel. It is there in that phrase that we have rather loosely translated as peace and rest. It comes after the section about the demands of being a disciple of Christ and what it means for us in our life.

Jesus says: 'Come to me all who are weary' – and that is all of us.' Lay your burdens at my feet and take my yoke upon you, my concerns. If you are faithful in these, you will find a rest and a peace deep in your soul.' The peace and the rest for which our souls cry out.

Amen.

Sermon 8

The Rocks of the Church

21 August 2005

Matthew 16:13–20

I have a thing about questionnaires. I do not like them. It is not so much the questions, but what you do with the answer. I had a friend who asked his congregation: 'Do you like music as it is?' or (in the other box) 'Do you like different music?' Of the replies, 51 per cent ticked one box, 49 per cent ticked the other. There seems nothing wrong with the question; but can you cope with the answer, with the expectation you create, and can you meet it?

One of the first recorded questionnaires took place on the road to Caesarea Philippi. Jesus asked his disciples two questions. The first was, 'Who do people say I am?' The disciples answered the question with some stock answers. 'Some say John the Baptist, some say Elijah, others say one of the prophets.' Mere chit-chat in the street; but then Jesus asked the second question: 'Never mind what other people say. The church will not be built on what other people say. I ask *you* this question. Who do *you* say I am?' That is the nub of the story. We know what happened when Peter answered in the way he did. He blurted out: 'You are the Christ, the son of the living God'. This was the answer that prompted Jesus to say to Peter: 'You are the rock, and upon you I will build my church'.

Now, we are not going to go down the lines of apostolic succession, because Matthew 16 has nothing to do with that. It was not Peter as an individual who was given the great task of being the cornerstone of the church. It was the answer. We know what the relationship was like between Jesus and Peter. We know how often Jesus chastised him for his lack of faith, for getting it wrong, for missing the point. These are hardly criteria for being the cornerstone of the church! So, let us set aside the apostolic succession. It was the reply to that question which prompted Jesus to say: 'On you I will build my church'. I would claim that, depending on our answer to that same question, Jesus will say the same. 'Upon you I will build my church.'

The rock of its members' confessions

So, what is it then that the Church is built on? I would suggest firstly that the Church is built on the rock of the confessions of its members. Peter said: 'You are the Christ, the son of the living God'. Jesus responded: 'Upon you I will build my church because of what you have said'. The person of Jesus, even at the beginning of his ministry, when he was relatively unknown, still had this impact on people. They talked about him, they wondered about who he was. Perhaps they realised that, in some ways, he defied description – which leaves us the task of trying to say who he is.

'Who do men say I am? But who do you say I am?' It is a question that has perplexed Christians and non-Christians alike for centuries. As at Caesarea Philippi, the Church will not rest and the Church will not be built on public opinion, but on the confession of you and me. One writer put it this way: 'For the first Christians, Jesus was not one solution among many. He is the solver. He was not one branch of the way, one aspect of the truth, one expression of life. He was The Way, The Truth and The Life. It was as they realised that, and experienced it in their lives, that Peter was able to reply to that question, "You are the Christ, the son of the living God".' It was on that confession that the church was built, and it was on that confession the church will stand.

I think it is fair to say that, when Jesus said 'On you I will build my church', he did not, in any sense, have in mind the organisation that we have inherited. In some respects, that does not matter. We use 'the Church' in its best and truest sense, when it refer to the coming together of those who worship God, the gathering of that very special community of such different people, united in their belief, and in their desire to worship and serve God. There is a sense in which it does not matter what buildings we build, or what organisation we have, however dear they are to us. By 'Church', we mean that body of Christian men and women who claim to be his disciples, so that, as individuals and corporately, when they come together and confess Jesus Christ as Saviour and Lord, it is on that confession that the Church was built, it is on that confession that the Church will stand.

The rock of their changed lives

The second thing I would say to you is this. The Church was also built on the transformed lives of those who made that confession. If our words and our actions do not match up, then 'hypocrite' is the word that comes to mind, and it is the word that the world will throw at us. In all honesty, if it is true, we should catch it. If what we say and what we do are not matching, then our faith is in danger. Peter, unnerved by panic, who denied his Master when he needed him most, suddenly after the Crucifixion became the driving force of that small nucleus that became the

Church. By the power of the Spirit, he showed the courage and commitment necessary of his people.

Our words and our actions must match, however frail we think we are. You know, and I know, that we are talking not about the Ten Commandments but about the much greyer, in-between area of our daily lives.

I think I have to share with you my favourite story of a little child drawing a very imaginative summer picture, and the girl's father said: 'Where did you get all these fancy coloured pens?' She said: 'I brought them from school'. 'You must not do that,' he said, 'that is stealing. If you want pens, I will bring them from the office.' We laugh, but we laugh because it touches a nerve. If our actions do not match our words, then our faith is in vain.

Our Church is built on the faith of our members. Here in the security and comfort of the church, we can confess much together. For, in that sense, we are like-minded. However, it is *how* we live our lives when we go from this place that matters. The Church was built on the confession of its members and will continue to be built on that confession.

I would also suggest to you that it is built on the changed lives of those who made that confession. If it has not changed us in any way, then what is the point? That is not to say we do not fall from grace, for nobody knows ourselves better than we do. We are not perfect. We seek and we strive and we know how often we fall and we fail. We pick ourselves up and we realise that, when the fall has been hardest, someone else has picked us up. We turn and receive God's word of forgiveness and we journey on, but always attempting to be his people. We are called to live out in our lives the words we say so easily and glibly with our lips. Built on the clear confession of its members, built on the changed lives of those who make that confession, the Church will grow and develop.

The rock of God's purpose

The final thing I would like to say to you is this. Perhaps, in some ways, it is the one that underpins them all. I would suggest to you that the Church was built on the rock of God's purpose. Let us never imagine that the Church is a purely human invention. Much of the outward sign is; our buildings, our liturgy and our hymns often reflect the great figures and personalities of the past. We are inheritors of a tradition; and sometimes, with a good deal of difficulty and pain, we try to express that in our own time and generation, so that the eternal Word might speak.

We know that this is not the whole story, that the Church is not a human invention of like-minded individuals trying to be good. It is responding to the call of God because this is part of this purpose. If you consider how universal the Church is, it is quite astonishing that it saw the first light of day at all. Yet, from that very small, frightened, ancient band of Jews, we have a Christian faith that has crossed frontiers, cultures and languages. It finds itself at home in the ancient world as well as the modern age. How do we explain that except in terms that it is part of the purpose of God?

Even all our attempts to be 'the Church' have not frustrated us. Perhaps that explains its great resilience. When suffering persecution, she stood the test. When torn apart by internal corruption and division, she stood the test. When faced with the apathy and indifference of so many, she stood the test. The Church has emerged from generation after generation to meet the challenge of its day. Sometimes it is unrecognisable from the past, but still the people of God who gather for worship call themselves 'the Church'.

If you had been in Jerusalem at the time of the Crucifixion when they took Christ down from the Cross and put him in the tomb, how long would you have given the Christian Church? If you had lived at the time of the Reformation, if you saw the corruption and politics of all sides at work, how long would you have given the Christian Church?

If you had lived in the sophisticated days of the Enlightenment, the Industrial Revolution with all its moves forward, its ascendancy over us as individuals, the denouncement of Christianity as ancient and irrelevant amid all the sophistication of the age, how long would you have given the Christian Church?

Yet we are still here. Perhaps the Church is here because and in spite of us, not because it is our invention, but because it is part of the purpose of God. 'You are the Christ', said Peter, 'Son of the living God.' In response to that, Jesus said: 'You are the rock, and upon you I will build my church'. It is built on the rock of the confession of its members, built on the rock of the changed lives of those who made that confession, built on the rock that is the purpose of God.

Amen.

Sermon 9

Challenging Words
for Tough Times

24 April 2005

John 14:1–14

The challenge of language is never far away from the preaching of the Word. Illustrations and analogies used in biblical times may not have the same import now. Indeed, some words and phrases might have quite a different and inappropriate meaning. Imagine those taking the gospel to people for the first time. When they took the gospel to the cannibals of New Guinea and said: 'Jesus said, "This is my body which is for you"'. Imagine going to parts of India and saying 'Jesus is the bread of life' when bread was expensive, a luxury for the rich, when rice was the staple diet.

The challenge of language is greatest at the time of Easter when we are dealing with images and analogies to which we might struggle to relate in our day and age. All the talk of empty tombs and of angels and of gardeners and of not recognising people on the road to Emmaus is confusing. However, surely when I opened the readings for this Sunday, John 14, surely now we have reached somewhere where language is not an issue, where this most wonderful of readings simply speaks for itself? The language is so beautiful and so clear that I thought: 'Why not have a different sermon; why do I not just read the lesson again and sit down'. That is rhetorical!

> Let not your hearts be troubled, neither let them be afraid. In my Father's house there are many mansions. If it were not so, I would have told you. And I go to prepare a place for you. And if I go and prepare a place for you, I will come again and take you to myself, so that where I am you may be also. Peace is my parting gift to you. My own peace such as the world cannot give. Set your troubled hearts at rest and banish your fears.

There can be few lovelier passages in Scripture. Perhaps also, on first reading, this is a passage needing no kind of explanation. The disciples hear Jesus speaking about Jesus' death. Despite all the challenges, they are having the time of their lives with him. The thought of not being with him makes them anxious and afraid. This is, in John's gospel, just after Jesus washes the disciples' feet before he goes to his Crucifixion. He needs to tell them the reality of the situation they are in. Perhaps he could see by their faces what it meant to them. They were then anxious and afraid:

- this is not the way it is meant to be …
- this is not the future we imagined …

Who knows, perhaps in this touching moment Jesus decided this because of the reaction. 'Let not your hearts be troubled, neither let them be afraid.'

In this wonderful passage from John's gospel, I want to suggest *three aspects* that he was mentioning to the disciples which I think speak to us now. While we say that these are wonderful, beautiful, charming words, there are also some very difficult words in among these fourteen verses.

I want first of all to say something about *many mansions*. Jesus said: 'In my Father's house there are many rooms, and if it was not so I would have told you. I am going to prepare a place for you, and if I go and prepare a place, I will come again and take you to myself, that where I am you may be also.' I think it is a word of continuity. It is a word to the disciples that the life of faith in Christ is not limited by the time we spend on earth.

The relationship that the disciples have had with Christ will not end either when Christ dies or when they die. This eternal life is something we can experience now when we live on beyond death – it is continuity. In all the places we have lived together, here is Jesus saying: 'But there's also plenty of room in my Father's house, and we will be there together'. It is a word of continuity; it is a word that reminds people that this life in Christ is not simply a promise of pie in the sky when we die, but simply the continuation of that life in Christ in a different realm.

That is the reason that this passage is more often than not used at funerals. It is because it reminds us of that continuity. I used it yesterday in the chapel here. We had the most moving memorial service. I say that, not because of anything I said, but because of what the deceased's brother said. We were giving thanks for the life of Edgar Chirambo, whose daughter Gertrude worships regularly with us in St Columba's.

Fourteen of the family were here yesterday; the remainder are all still in Malawi, where Edgar died. They wanted simply to have the opportunity to give thanks for his life, and I read these words. What moved me were the words of his brother Chester. It was a different culture. It was good to be reminded exactly why we were having the service. It was very simple; English is not his first language. He gave thanks to God for the life of Edgar, and on behalf of the family, thanked God for Edgar giving them all discipline and love and the Christian faith. There were no endless eulogies about his life, about his low handicap at golf, his love of the hills. That was it: his discipline, his love and his faith that he gave to his family.

There was also no mention of the cutting short of his life because their expectation was different. He was 56 when he died, and in Malawi that is not bad. So, they were able to give thanks without any feelings of injustice or hurt. He said: 'My brother knew when he was ill that it was time to go home and to be with Jesus'. In our terribly clever Western way, when ministers construct services, to say that all he wanted to do was to go home and be with Jesus is not something we would express. However, that is what it says.

It was good for the family, and it was also good for the minister to hear the power and the simplicity of that family's faith in the continuity of the gospel. He had gone to be with Christ, and one day they would be reunited. Now, I would suggest that this word of continuity is something that people need to hear. What Jesus established here on earth and by his dying and rising again is continued in his presence forever. The point at which we share that same life in a different way will sadly vary tremendously in our lives. However, it does not negate the promises that Jesus made. It is a word of continuity.

The second thing I want to say is this phrase: *'No-one comes to the Father except by me'*. This is a well-beloved phrase of many of our more zealous Christians:

- it is a phrase used to put an end to any kind of interfaith dialogue;

- an end to all this talk that everybody is walking up the same mountain;

- a condemnation of any approach suggesting that it does not matter what faith you have;

- a rejection of any notion that we are all walking up a different side, but when we get to the top we will all meet each other.

'No,' say some Christians, 'the gospel is quite clear; salvation is only through Christ. No-one comes to the Father except by me. Only those who embrace Christ will be saved.' They may be right. However, I was more struck by one writer who tried to put this into the context in which it was said. The phrase 'No-one comes to the Father except by Christ' was not spoken to those who were not Christians as a tool of evangelism. This was not something to beat people over the head with. They say: 'By the way, if you want to avoid the fiery pit, Christ is the only way'.

This was used to the Christian community themselves. I think it was uttered and recorded to say: 'Do you recognise your distinctiveness? Do you recognise the unique thing to which you have been called?' The writer said: 'Even then and now, if someone came from outer space, would they be able to tell the difference between the social and political climate of the day and the secular religion and the Church, because of its priorities, because of its criteria, because of how it measures its health and strength?'

What is the distinctiveness of the Church? This was directed at Christians, not non-Christians. If that continuity is a word that many need to hear, this is something that we need to hear. The words were not given to the faithful to pass on to the world to say 'This is the only way'. It was given to those who are the Church to say: 'Do you recognise the distinctiveness of what you have been given? You must stand over and against the world even though we live in it. We do not absorb the standards of the world, nor adapt ourselves to the morality of the world.' In some cases, that is not saying because the world's morality has slipped, but in some cases the world is more draconian and unforgiving than Christ. It is the distinctiveness of those living in Christ, both here and in the life to come. That is a word I believe the Church needs to hear. What makes us different? It is our life in Christ and nothing else.

At the end of the passage, Jesus says to his disciples: *'Ask what you will in my name* and you will receive it'. The crucial thing in that phrase is 'in my name'. This is not a kind of ranting over the indulgences and cravings of children. Nor is it in any kind of natural, if selfish, way to ask God to do what we want in order to put the world to rights. It comes at the end; if we recognise this continuity of our life in Christ. If we recognise the distinctiveness of his people, with his message and the challenge of the gospel, it is then that we turn our minds to the world and ask in his name. If we do that, Jesus says we will receive it.

We often hear that:

- that miracles are something to be scorned at,

- that miraculous things are of the past,

- that the stories we relate are always ancient stories,

- that the Church is somehow an amalgamation of people who enjoy looking back and sharing old stories.

It is a reminder that God is still at work and active in his Church. It is the only thing that will change this Sacrament from a rather meagre offering of afternoon tea into Holy Communion. That Christ is present with his people. That in and through his Church and in and through us as individuals he is still active, he can still do things. This is a live body of Christ. 'Ask what you will in my name. Be faithful to what I have given you, be faithful to the challenge of the gospel, and I will still do great things in and through you.' It is a word of continuity in a world that thinks death is the end. It is a word where the Church can so easily be absorbed into the world in which it is set, to remind us of our distinctiveness in Christ and what we have to offer. It is a reminder that God is still active in and through his people and can still surprise us. I think the crucial factor now is not 'Do people understand that?' It is 'Do they believe it?'

Some years ago, friends of mine who lived in a major city in the UK adopted two children from a children's home. The children were a fairly advanced age for adoption – they might have been five and seven. Damage had been done, and life was very hard. One of the great things they remember the children speaking about, coming out of an institution and going into a family home, was the fact that they had their own room. I recall this when reading John 14, 'In my Father's house there are many rooms, and I go and prepare a place for you', because of the security of knowing that they were wanted.

However, did these children believe it? They embarked upon a programme of doing everything they could to destroy that relationship. As the children grew, they destroyed the rooms. They destroyed some of their possessions that were very dear to our friends. They broke into the church which meant everything to our friends. The psychologist and the psychiatrist said: 'What is at the root here is that they understand what has happened, they understand that you have adopted them, they understand that this is now their home, but do they really believe it? Is there anything they can do and say that would destroy that? Are you going to hand them back? Is this going to give them the continuity that their lives crave? Are you going to be strong enough not simply to give them what they want so that they might love you?'

In the life of the Church;

- Do we believe what we can easily understand – that death is not the end, that Jesus here is offering the continuity of life with him, here and in the life to come?

- Do we believe in the distinctiveness of the Church?

- Do we have the courage to declare that distinctiveness and not to back off from it because we feel under pressure, or embarrassment, in a sophisticated world that seems to have left the Church behind?

- Do we believe that God will still answer our prayers by having our best interests at heart, if we genuinely pray in his name – not simply give us what we want so that we might believe in him?

The challenge to the Church – the early Church, the challenge to our friends and their fragile family is our challenge. Jesus said: 'I am the way, the truth and the life'. We understand it, but do we believe it? That is the question.

Amen.

Parables of Jesus

Sermon 10

The Good Samaritan

11 July 2003

Luke 10:25–37

Our all-age summer service is in full flow, and this morning at 9:30 we acted out the parable of the Good Samaritan. At no insignificant cost, I played the priest.

- What do we do with the Good Samaritan?

- Is there any better-known part of Scripture?

- Is there anything more oft-quoted when we feel good about the half an hour a year we have given to the poor? We have done our Good Samaritan bit.

- So, what is it saying to us?

- Is it saying: do not walk past people in the street?

- Is it just about an act of kindness?

When Chad Varah founded his telephone service, he called it the Samaritans. In a sense, we have come full circle, because some insurance for doctors now has a Good Samaritan clause, and they call it that. That is: if you stop and help someone in the street and you do not do it right, they can sue you. Such is the world in which we live.

Suddenly I realised, in my brief time in London, how easy it is to skirt over this first very obvious reading of the Good Samaritan. We are not going to spend long on it, but let us not decry that moment of stopping in the street

– because few of us do it, and I count myself one of them. We have become astonishingly inventive as to why we do not stop:

- we are in a rush, we should not speak to strangers,
- we are going somewhere else,
- it is their own fault,
- they will only buy alcohol,
- there are plenty of hostels.

So, what is the point?

We rampage through all these thoughts as possible reasons for walking past without any idea that even a pound coin might be worth the risk. We will be conned for a much bigger amount than that in the course of a week. We do walk past people lying in the streets of our great city. So,

- if you do not like anything else I am going to say,
- if you feel anything else is a bit contrived,

just hold on to that in the week that lies ahead and have the faith and take the risk just to stop for a moment.

I stood at a bus stop in Oxford Street recently, and there was a man sitting, as they often do, next to the cash machine in case something should fall out of someone's pocket. We were all standing there looking at this man across the street, racking up the sympathy, as he sat with a well-behaved Doberman pup wrapped in a blanket beside him. An elderly lady stopped and engaged him in a conversation which we obviously could not hear. She walked on. A few minutes later, she returned. She had gone into Starbucks and had bought a sandwich which she gave to him.

But the story is more than just that. Duncan was one of our youngsters on family duty this morning. I asked who wanted to play the person who had been mugged. The walk-on, walk-off, lying-on-the-carpet part appealed to Duncan, so he lay on the carpet clutching an umbrella I had given him.

We moved on to the next stage of the story in which we tried to imagine how we could bring the story up to date and not lose the radical, outrageous message that Jesus has given. So Duncan opened his umbrella, and on it, was written Rangers Football Club. Now, someone has already said this morning: 'He deserved to be mugged!' – so do not tell me at the door, because I have already heard it at half past nine! Who do you think stopped? 'A Celtic supporter', someone said. We laugh, but just for a moment; it is beginning to capture what this story is all about. It does not go far enough, as we shall see, but at least it is a stage beyond this idea of flicking fifty pence in the hat.

Suddenly, it is speaking to us about risk, about vulnerability, about doing something other people think is wrong, not about what is expected, not the kind of people with whom you would associate. Now, that at least preserves the thrust of the characters of this story. The priest and the Levite walked past; but it is not just anyone who stopped, it is the Samaritan. In a West of Scotland context, unless we keep that Glasgow Celtic and Rangers thing in mind, we lose the impetus of what it was to have the ultimate outsider stop:

- the most hated minority group in the ancient part of the world,

- the very group with whom the Jews would have no truck whatsoever. They would not even walk on the same side of the road as the Samaritans.

So, Jesus is making the point that it is the Samaritan who stops.

The Jews were living in a world where kith and kin were everything. Family came first. Few of us would argue with that. However, they could extend that family to such an extent that they could justify on religious grounds the most outrageous behaviour to others, if it was to protect the family. Then there was the outside layer in this archer's target, of those who are perhaps your servants and other acceptable ethnic groups. The Samaritans were not even on the board. In another way, Jesus is trying to say: 'Can you break out of this mould?' It is the Samaritan who stops. He is saying: 'You must extend your concept of the Kingdom because it includes them as well'. We could spend ages trying to relate this to modern-day Samaritans, but you know them as well as I do. You watch the television, you read the newspapers, you know well those who are thought of as being beyond the pale.

You know the challenge, but the thrust of the story lies with the priest and the Levite. They have had a raw deal, the priest and the Levite. They have somehow become the butt of this: 'Do not be like them'. But we are all like them, and the reason is that this is a story about racism: deep-seated, institutionalised, traditional racism.

What the priest and the Levite did by walking by was what was expected of them. Under Jewish law, priests and Levites were not allowed to go near or touch dead bodies, not even their own parents. What a different complex the story takes now! This is no longer hard-hearted priest and Levite, too busy, too proud to go near the body; they were not allowed. That is institutional racism. They had built into the fabric of their employment what was expected of them in terms of what they should and should not do with others. So, in a sense there is a double whammy in this story: not only on the one hand is it the Samaritan who offers the help, but on the other, it is exposing how easy it is to make racism acceptable.

It is being done by religious people.

- The theologians and leaders of the Dutch Reformed Church managed on their own rather sideways biblical interpretation to justify apartheid.

- The southern states of America in the pre-Civil Rights era were rife with black people being hanged for no reason by those who would populate the church on a Sunday.

- What is happening now is that insidiously we are being driven in the same way so that somehow whole nations and whole ethnic groups are out because of the activities of some.

- Our children are growing up in a world where they are encouraged to see Islam as a world threat in itself, and that those who share this faith are a threat to Christianity and are not to be trusted.

- We have newspaper headlines calling entire nations 'animals'. It is a bit unfair on animals, which are not nearly as vindictive as we are.

This is a very powerful story that we have sanitised and made the Samaritan into some kind of secular saint, a byword for doing the odd good thing to those who are not as fortunate. It is a very powerful and, both for its day and for our own, a very shocking indictment of racism; that somehow because of your colour, because of your faith, because of the cultural context in which you live, you are 'in' or you are 'out'. That is the point of the story: the priest and the Levite did what was expected of them according to the law.

So, there is the challenge for Christian people to take the story of the Good Samaritan and to live it out in the world in which we live, where we are under pressure to narrow its boundaries. Jesus is saying that the Kingdom of God bears no relation to the kingdom in which we now reside. It does not operate by the same rules. He says to us: 'You do not decide who is in and out' – and thank God for that, because could we be trusted?

That is not the same as saying that the activities of everyone in the world are acceptable. There is an evil in the world that needs to be combated, but the threat of evil is defined not by current international alignments, not by the decision of others, but according to the law of Christ:

- The killing of innocents, either by allied planes or by suicide bombers, is wrong.

- No-one is saying that 'anything goes', but the benchmark is the Kingdom of God that Jesus Christ came to bring.

- He is the one who is telling you to expand your view of the Kingdom of God to include those whom the world might find unacceptable.

It is not an easy message. It is not easy being a Good Samaritan:

- there are some who are astonishingly ungrateful;

- there are many who do not want our help;

- there are some people whom we try to help, and we get so much abuse that I am sure we go home and wonder why we bother.

It is not an easy thing to do, it is not easy on a personal level, it is not easy as a nation, to grasp the Kingdom of God as defined in the ministry of Jesus Christ. For this is not an isolated story. Throughout his ministry; Jesus is constantly saying to the disciples: 'Look to the side of you, look to all the people who are on the margins of our society, the ones whom other people count as unworthy, beyond the pale, those who certainly are not due to be in the Kingdom of God'. These are the very ones whom he stops, touches and lifts and embraces and loves. It is one of the best-known stories. At its most superficial, it is one of the easiest to keep. I would suggest that, at its deeper level, it is one of the most challenging and the most shocking for any Christian generation and the one that could and should keep us awake the most.

Amen.

Sermon 11

The Forgiving Father

21 March 2004

Luke 15:1–3, 11b–32

If there is a theme which links our three readings today, it is surely the restoring power of the love of God. The verses we read from Joshua told, in very understated terms, of Israel's final release from all those years of bondage in Egypt and their first celebration of the Passover in freedom. Just that one line *'There was no longer any manna because there was no longer any need'* is crucial. Now they would eat from the land of Canaan. God's love had not failed them. God's promise had been fulfilled. Despite all their experiences, despite all those moments when they must have imagined that God had abandoned them, here they were, still loved and safely in Canaan.

Paul's letter to the church in Corinth states: *'The old has gone, all is new because of what God has achieved in Christ'*. He has reconciled the world to himself through Christ's death and resurrection. We are called to share in that reconciliation. God loves us so much that he gave us his Son.

Now to our gospel reading. *'There was once a man who had two sons.'* Of all the passages in the Bible, surely this is one of the most well remembered. How often the Prodigal Son has been preached about – and the challenge for the preacher is always this. What can we say about the

Prodigal Son that we have not said before? In some of the background reading I was doing, I came across a writer who said: 'Simply to tell the story is to preach the gospel afresh'. I have not chosen the Prodigal Son as my title. That is the popular title, but in all my reading I found it rarely referred to as 'the Prodigal Son'. Most of the other titles refer to the father:

- the forgiving father
- the loving father
- the waiting father.

There are clearly three characters, and each plays his part. However, central to the story is the father.

Let us begin with the younger son. He takes the initiative. It is the younger son who starts it off, demanding what was his so that he can go off and party. The details we do not know are unimportant. What we do know about Jewish inheritance law is that he would inherit a fraction of what his older brother would inherit. Given the fact that they had farmlands and servants, they were clearly wealthy. Therefore, even the younger brother's small portion would still be enough with which to party. Off he goes and squanders it. Children have a lovely, refreshing way of telling the story. One Sunday School child wrote: 'The Prodigal Son, he got his money, he spent most of it on wine and women and then he wasted the rest'. It will depend very much on your theology whether you agree with that or not.

The text just says wild living, but the original says 'inappropriate behaviour', whatever that means. It is the elder brother who introduces the prostitutes; and he can hardly be considered an objective viewer of his younger brother's behaviour. Clearly the younger brother enjoyed himself, he spent it all, he ended up in the most abhorrent position, and no modern translation can lose the impact of a Jewish person's only job being to feed pigs. Then, in that glorious understatement, he came to his senses, and he decided that he needed to go back. He recognised his own situation, and realised just how far he had slipped. There was nothing else for it – he would need to go home.

Then we move to the father. The son rehearses his speech. He is going to be contrite, he is going to be very sorry, he is even going to offer to be one of the hired servants. He had done so badly, he did not even expect to get back to the position he was in before, but anything was better than this. What about the father's recognition of his position? The crucial thing here, which is why we have said the forgiving father, rather than the loving father, or the waiting father, is the father's recognition that what is happening does not stand, or fall, on the son's attitude. The forgiveness and the love which the father shows is not dependent on how contrite the son is. No – while the younger son is still far off, the father runs to him with the sheer joy of seeing his son come back.

The son might have been coming back to ask for a top-up; children do that, you know. He might have been saying he had gone through it, he had learned his lesson; give him a bit more and he will do better. Who knows what is in the son's mind? Certainly, the father does not. Just the act of coming back is enough. He runs to him and he kisses him, he embraces him, and well we know the story of what he plans. Both the father and the son are found. Can there be anything better than the father reunited with the son?

Yet the father's actions would not be without their critics. Those hearing the story for the first time would say: 'Wealthy Jewish fathers do not do that. How undignified. They do not run anywhere.' Surely, for the father to retain something of his dignity and self-respect, he would at least wait until the son crawled in through the door. 'What have you got to say for yourself?' would be a good line. Then, perhaps somewhat grudgingly, he would say: 'Well, I will take you back as long as you have learned your lesson'. Not an unreasonable thing to say. Only when the father feels that the son is contrite enough will he allow him in the back door, without any promises for the future. Yet none of that happens. He throws the party with unmitigated joy, no strings attached – just the sheer joy that the son is back.

The story would be fine if it ended there; but of course it does not. There is the older brother. One commentary I read paints a very bleak picture, an astonishingly naïve, picture and in many ways a very inaccurate picture, but an easy one to paint. The younger son is like those who are outside the Church – a common theme for preachers. The older son is like those in the Church who are extremely upset at the prospect of any of the promises of God being extended to those whose lifestyle is abhorrent, or whose views they do not share and whose dress, to say the least, is quirky. It is not about that. It is about the father.

There is a very touching moment and a very under-standable moment when the older brother cannot see the natural justice in the story. He does not storm in and complain, he just stays away. He finds out from a servant what is happening; he does not kick the door down and say to his father: 'What do you think you are doing?' He just feels excluded. He feels wronged. It is the father who finds him. The father, when he hears, does not say to the servant: 'Just give him space, let him come to terms with it. It must be a bit of a shock, his brother coming back. Just let him get used to the idea. He will be fine.' The father does not scold or patronise the older brother.

As he did with the younger one, he goes out to find him. The initiative lies with the father, and he restates his case. The older son tells him about his feelings of injustice, how he feels he never had any of the things that the younger brother is getting. The father listens and does not chide him for his selfishness. He loves him. 'Everything I have is yours. You are with me always. Nothing has changed. What I feel for your brother, I feel for you.' What the older brother does then, we have no idea. Only in Hollywood are there happy endings, for that is not the point.

The point is: whoever you identify with, whether you sometimes feel you are the younger brother, or the older, does not really matter. What we are here to hear again and to share is not our pettiness, not our wastefulness, not our fits of pique, but God's love for us. We are all there somewhere, from someone who drinks away a small fortune in wild living at one end of the spectrum, to the pursed lips of someone who thinks they are perfect and deserves everything God has to give. We are all in there somewhere.

The crucial nature of this story is: wherever we are in that spectrum, and we are not always in the same place, God's forgiving love reaches out to us. That is the point of the story, not to make those who are outside the Church feel guilty, and those who are inside the Church feel smug:

- It is about the forgiving love of God which knows no limits, whoever comes to him.

- We are all there somewhere, between the bookends of the sons.

- Wherever we are in that shelf, and we will move from one end to the other as we go through our lives, the crucial thing is the father.

- God in Christ has reconciled the world to himself

- That while we were yet sinners, Christ died for us.

That is what the parable says, that while he was still far off, unable to tell his story, or make his excuses or promises which he might or might not be able to keep, God went out to him, threw his arms round him and embraced him. Then he went out to find the older too, in his fit of pique and jealousy. Thinking you are lost in the sight of God is not about distance. The loving, forgiving father welcomed back the son from another country. He also welcomed back the older brother who was also lost, but who had never left home.

Amen.

The Shrewd Manager

19 September 2004

Luke 16:1–13

Twenty-five years ago, I was the minister in my first parish in the sunny Ayrshire coastal town of Saltcoats. In my congregation at Saltcoats, I had a tax-collector, and he used to say to me: 'If the reading contains my profession, will you let me know, because I am tired of it and I am not a sinner'. In the full flush of confident youth, I said: 'You are a sinner, but not because of your tax-collecting'. However, that was a distinction lost on him. I tried to explain to him that, in the world in which the first-century people lived, tax-collecting meant something completely different. As I said that, his eyes glazed over, and it did not really make much difference, because people still said: 'Here is the sinner coming'.

Today's reading comes not in isolation, but as part of a group of readings in Luke's gospel about this whole question of money and possessions. We have said, time and time again, that Jesus is not saying it is sinful to have these things. What can be sinful is the way we use them.

Our progress through Luke's gospel brings us to today's very awkward story. I have to say that what I offer you today is not in agreement with everyone I have read. In all the commentaries and books we refer to when we are preparing, there are many opinions about this strange reading in which Jesus seems to give his blessing to sharp practice. Most commentators are agreed that the three great statements that follow probably come from a different time and have been added to try to give some weight to this story about shrewd, or dishonest, management. These are the ones that come at the end, the ones that say:

> 'If you are dishonest with small things, you will be dishonest with the large things.' 'If you cannot be trusted with money, how will you be trusted with real riches?' 'You cannot serve God and money.'

Each of these almost demands a sermon in its own right.

Today, however, we are going to concentrate on this very strange story about the manager. The first thing we have to do, as we often have to do with these biblical stories, is try to put it in some context. What would be the world-view of people hearing it for the first time? The story seems strange to us for a number of reasons, until we think of the context of that first-century world.

The first thing to say is that the manager had not been doing anything that he was not allowed to do. Managers made their money, as tax-collectors did, by adding their own commission. Sometimes that could be crippling. The tax-collector was told to collect a certain amount of taxes for the temple, or for Caesar; but it was all on commission, and the tax-collector could add whatever he wanted by way of his own cut. As you can imagine; this was a recipe for dishonesty and malpractice; and, for that reason, tax-collectors are numbered with sinners in the Bible. However, the same was true of those who sold produce. The manager could charge commission which, at that time, for something as expensive as olive oil, was 100 per cent. The commission for something a little more common, like wheat, was 25 per cent.

Now, read that back into the story. Suddenly we realise then that this story takes on a different character. What the manager is actually doing is giving up his profit, recognising that there is a debt that needs to be paid, but only for the most selfish motives. He is going to try to endear himself to those who are in debt by giving up his commission. This is what makes it a strange and challenging story. It is all motivated by self-interest.

There is that marvellous part when he realises the game is up, and his source of income might disappear. He reflects: 'I am not strong enough to work and I am too proud to beg'. Desperate situations require desperate measures. In the hope of endearing himself to those to whom he might have to go for charity, he apparently cancels a large proportion of their debt, and he is commended for it. If there is any passage in Scripture that reminds us that the gospel is part of the real world, it is this one. If there is any part of Scripture that is an antidote to the Sermon on the Mount, it is this one. If there is any antidote to the idea that the Christian faith simply holds out an impossible ideal before us to which we can try to measure up, and therefore is simply a constant source of guilt and disappointment, it is this one.

Blessed are the pure in heart, blessed are the pure in spirit. Does that apply to anyone here in St Columba's this morning? Always the gospel is presented as the perfect ideal which we miserably strive to achieve but constantly fail. Here is a reminder that God in Christ came to the world, sinful as it is, because the world matters to him. That is why Jesus said: 'Now I send you out into the world like sheep among wolves. Be wary as serpents, and be innocent as doves.' It is a story about debt, about self-interest, about compromise – and, if that is not a story about the world in which we are set, about the world in which we are called to be his disciples, then I do not know what is.

The heart of the story is about selfishness. Now, we may like to get caught up in this man's motives. It is an easy way of avoiding the thrust of the story, which is that the man in the story, and we ourselves, ultimately have to do with less. The world will not sustain our level of consumption, and there is no delicate, caring, sharing way of saying that. We are consuming too much, and what we are consuming affects other people. Not only is this man giving up his excessive, selfish part of the deal, but in doing so he reduces someone else's debt.

Some commentators would like to spiritualise the story. They concentrate on the man's motives. I think Jesus is saying to us, in a response that is full of irony, full of pathos, that he does not care what the motives are.

You try telling the 500,000 children who die every year in our world through hunger that we are not sending the food because we are not quite sure about the motives of those who are giving it.

You try telling those who are waiting for tents and blankets to be dropped, because they have suffered from a hurricane, that the planes will be delayed because we are not really quite sure about the motives of the governments who are sending them.

Questioning the motives comes from a Western privileged tradition that has enough and is too often used as a cop-out for help.

Jesus praised the manager, and I think he praised him because he was doing something, he was facing up to his responsibilities and he was removing that dreadful level of selfishness from this equation. If that does not speak to our world, I do not know what does.

It is a difficult and challenging story because giving away all that we have to those who have not is not the answer, and it never has been. The Church stopped preaching that message forty years ago because it was getting us nowhere;

it was clouding the issue. My mother was always irritated when we were at children's parties and someone said: 'You are not going to finish that, are you? Just think of all the starving children in Africa.' So I would finish it, as if my gluttony was going to do something about the starving children. It does not work that way, but that is what we teach children with that message.

It is much more subtle than that. It is about asking Christian people to engage in the Christian processes of the world; it is having Christian people at the heart of politics and at the heart of commerce, and at the very heart of business, so that we might bring a Christian ethos into what we do. It is not saying that having these things is necessarily bad, or painting a medieval picture of theology by telling us to give them away. How can we use them, how can our generosity, how can our hard work in a Christian sense benefit those who have nothing? We are fellow pilgrims on a common journey.

In our modern world, there is the challenge – the challenge of Christian service in a world

- where often profit is everything,
- when those who have, have access to more,
- which often sees people's worth in terms of what they have accumulated,
- where people are desperate and not always interested in our motives. You are not concerned about motives if you are starving and you are homeless.

These ancient readings are more profound and more subtle than we could ever imagine. They are not here to induce guilt. They are not here to say to those who have: 'You are the problem'. Instead, they are there to say: 'You are the solution'. Jesus went to weddings. He enjoyed meals. He himself was from a middle-class background. He dined with the scribes and the Pharisees and those who had much. The thrust of his message, in all the variety of these stories, is not that possession is sinful, but that selfishness is. Luke wrote these words 2,000 years ago. How can we say that the gospel does not really apply to and challenge the world in which we live today?

One final point: could this story tell us as much about the wealthy owner as it does about the manager? Does it not show the understanding and the generosity of the owner, who, far from condemning the manager, told him he was still part of the purpose of God?

Amen.

Sermon 13

The Two Sons

29 September 2002

Matthew 21:23–32

'But Dad, you promised' – words spoken to me by my daughter when she was five. She had just started school, the first form performance was due, Mums were expected, Dads were allowed, and I was not there. I had said I would be, but I never made it.

We are going to have three different looks at this parable today. Not three attempts to get it right, but three different perspectives on it.

I

Let us look at it firstly as a parable about being reliable, doing what you said you would do. On that level, no-one will argue about how important that is. Much of our frustration at waiting in for tradespeople is not the fact that the fridge was not repaired, but that we wasted a whole day because they said they would come. We live in an age when people do not trust the words that we say.

Many of you will remember that marvellous programme, 'Yes Minister', followed by 'Yes Prime Minister'. Jim Hacker, as the MP, is determined to do what he has promised to do. He finds the resistance of his Civil Servant difficult because he had made undertakings in his manifesto. His Civil Servant promptly reminds him that, while this is true, it is not something to be concerned about, because everyone understands that what appears in a manifesto is a political promise, and, therefore, is there to be broken.

We live in an age where we consume and emit words by the bucketload, and they have, in a sense, become devalued. How precious it is to have someone on whom we can rely. So the parable is telling us a story, a very simple story about two sons, *'Yes, I will do it'* and *'No, I will not.'* The one who said he would did not fulfil his promise. It is a parable about reliability.

II

Let us look again at that same parable in the context in which Jesus is speaking and in which Matthew records it. Let us focus for a moment on some of the characters who put a different light on what might be viewed simply as a parable about being reliable and keeping to your word.

Firstly, what was expected of the sons was not un-reasonable. The sons stand in a special relationship with the father, and working in the vineyard would seem to be their role in life. It was not an unusual expectation. Jesus wants to link the parable to those to whom he is speaking about authority and about entry into the Kingdom.

In some ways, the parable takes on a different character when we put it in its biblical setting, much wider, much deeper than simply reliability. 'By what authority are you doing and saying these things?' the authorities said to Jesus. As usual, in that irritating way, he does not answer; he gives this parable. Not only does he give the parable, but also he puts a question to those who had heard it. 'Which son do you think did the will of God?' The one who said he would, or the one who said he would not but did?

Then, at the end of the parable, we read Jesus' point. It is a very barbed criticism on the authorities of the day, the religious authorities who say they are going to do things, who profess with their lips in worship and in pronouncement, but do not deliver. Then the most cutting thing of all. Jesus said: 'Even those who eventually do it, whether they are prostitutes or tax-gatherers or sinners, they will enter the Kingdom before you'. Suddenly it takes on a much harsher reality than just being reliable. Suddenly it is saying to those of us who might profess with our lips, that unless we back it up with our actions, it is meaningless.

When Jesus met Peter on the shore at his resurrection appearance, he said three times to Peter: 'Do you love me?', and the response each time when Peter said 'You know that I love you' was not 'Well done, I am pleased to hear it'. He said: 'Feed my sheep'. Are you going to do what you profess?

In another place in Scripture, we are told that not everyone who says 'Jesus is Lord' will enter the Kingdom. Do you practise what you preach? We stand in that same relationship with God as the two sons did to the father. It is expected of us. As those who claim to be the disciples of Christ and who want to be his people, we need to move beyond the words that we say. Which of these two sons did the will of the father? The one who said he would not, or the one who found it easy to profess that he would do it, but failed? The failure comes:

- in saying one thing and doing another,
- of not matching our words with our actions,
- of not practising what we preach,
- of being able to come here into the atmosphere of worship and see the courage and the power while failing to go out and to profess in our lives what we so easily profess today with our lips.

III

Let us have a third look at the parable, in many ways a much harder look. Our second look at the parable could, in a sense, have been a division among the Christian people. There are some who say they will and will not, and there are some who say they cannot but they do. Take a more radical look at the parable, and just for a moment imagine that it is between people who are of the Christian faith and those who are not. Those who do not profess with their lips either because they do not want to or because they feel they do not need to. Think of the two sons as the division between those who profess the Christian faith and the rest of the world who do not. It becomes a harsh parable indeed, because what it is really saying to us is that God's purposes will not be thwarted and God will even use those who do not or cannot profess God's name.

We need look no further than the New Testament to see that Jesus was not particularly bound up with those who profess. Time and time again, in his parables and miracles, he used those who were not disciples, who were not professing their faith for whatever reason, who would not consider themselves in the inner circle, but were used by God in Christ for his purposes.

When Jesus is speaking of breaking down barriers of ethnic division, the incident happened with the Samaritan woman at the well, not in discussion with the disciples. When Jesus wanted to speak about what holds us back, about where we place our trust, he spoke to the rich young ruler, not to one of the disciples. It was an African who carried his Cross, not one of the twelve. Just think for a moment: if Jesus is really saying to us that it is important to be reliable, then it is important for Christian people to back up what they say for their credibility in the world, for what trips off the tongue in the atmosphere of worship spills out over the world where we are called to serve.

Even more, perhaps Jesus is also saying to us that it will be very regrettable if you do not do this, but my purposes will not be thwarted. Perhaps we have to acknowledge that others, who would not claim to be Christian, who would not want to be Christian, who would not want to sign up to our creed, or our worship, or our dogmas, are doing the will of God. People who are reaching those who are on the very margins of society, reaching out to those who others think are unacceptable; people who do not profess to be Christians, but in their lives are turning the other cheek, are the ones who are going the extra mile.

We have to recognise that the will of God might not be thwarted by our inability to match our actions with our words. Perhaps God does not recognise our divisions. I have never imagined that God is Presbyterian. God created the world and all that is in it, and that includes the son who would not profess, who would not commit, who would not say 'yes I will' but, in the living of his life, does do the will of God.

Perhaps you know people like that. I do. People who, through the sacrificial lives they lead, through their ability to reach out, touch those who need to be touched and forgiven and loved. Those who, at great cost to themselves, even to the cost of their own lives, have gone to places in the world we could not spell, let alone visit, and have shared with the hungry and with those who are oppressed. Those who have the courage to take to the streets about things they feel passionately about because they care for the world, yet who would not dream of calling themselves Christians, let alone consider occupying a pew. While we might regret that, while we might want them to be part of the fellowship here, they might still be doing the work of God.

Perhaps this parable is teaching us about humility, or reminding us that we do not have a monopoly on good works or the coming of the Kingdom. Perhaps it is calling us to recognise, to affirm and to support that work, where it is God's work, by those who will not or cannot profess with their lips his name. Is this biblical? Read again Matthew 21. Which one did the will of God?

Amen.

Christian Life

Radical or Respectable –
Inclusive or Exclusive?

27 February 2005

John 4:5–15, 27–30, 39–42

Mad dogs and Englishmen go out in the midday sun. To that we have to add the Samaritan woman and Jesus. Small wonder they found themselves alone at the well at a time of day when no-one in their right mind would go there. It is a part of a series of encounters we find in John's gospel. They consist not of detailed theological discussion but of encounters with real people. Last week it was Nicodemus, this week it is the Samaritan woman at the well. Next week it is the man born blind, the week after that it is Lazarus. These are real encounters trying to establish who this Jesus really is so that we may fully share the surprise of Easter. So, we come today to Jesus and the woman at the well.

We tried to give a little glimpse to the children of how radical this meeting really was. Samaritans were neither fish nor fowl. For historic reasons, the Jews considered them Gentiles and the Gentiles considered them Jews. It is small wonder that the word Samaritan appears at crucial times. In Luke's gospel, it is the Good Samaritan. The grateful leper, the only one of the ten who said thanks, was a Samaritan. The only other time it appears in John's gospel is when the authorities accuse Jesus himself of being a demon-possessed Samaritan.

In one sense, this story is full of symbolism. Nobody then would miss the symbolism of this happening at Jacob's well. Jacob had dreamt there was a ladder that would link heaven and earth – and, at that very same spot, heaven and earth are linked, not by some mystical ladder but by the presence of Jesus himself. The whole symbolism is of water, of purification and of thirst; the Old Testament is full of references to thirst being more than a physical thirst. In the Psalms and Lamentations, in the prophets, we hear: '*My soul thirsts for thee as a land parched and devoid of water*'. Samaritans and Jews have nothing to do with one another; the better translation is contained in the footnote at the bottom: '*they do not share vessels in common*'.

If there is one note we want to say about this reading, it is about the radical nature of this encounter. *Radical* is not a word we associated with Christians. However, the two words came together this week. There was a story in *The Times*, and other newspapers, about *Jerry Springer: The Opera*. I have not seen it, but I have seen *The Jerry Springer Show*, and it is so tedious that we shall just move on. What is important is what lies behind it. It is the whole furore about the opera and the blasphemy and the number of swear words; someone actually said 'if a swear word is repeated more than once, we only count it as one'. I am losing the will to live as I read this nonsense. But there comes the rub with this radical Christian group. How far we have slipped; but what does that say about the rest of us? Comfortable and safe, secure, constantly told not to get involved in politics, or the things of the world? We will be quite happy with you if you stay in your church and save souls.

Consider the new, radical Christian movement. There was a time when there was no need to say the word 'radical'. There was a time when saying the word 'Christian' meant 'radical'. History is full of the great occasions when we have moved forward, when we have done wild and courageous and brave things, when we have helped those who have been marginalised. The Church has often been at the forefront of breaking down walls of fear, suspicion and intolerance, being in the forefront of providing medicine and education.

There was a time when there was no need to say 'radical Christian'; but we are no longer radical, so we have left that phrase to the crazy minority. Now at least it is Christians and, although it is a type of Christianity with which I would rather not be associated, at least there is passion, at least they are moved to do and say something.

Christianity is radical. This is what this story is trying to say; it is the radical nature of what Jesus did. It cut across everything that everybody thought was respectable. However, 'respectable' is now a word that goes with Christianity. What Jesus did at that well cut across what everyone thought was safe. Now 'safe' is what we are about. What Jesus did at that well cut across everything people thought was hygienic – and that we certainly are.

How easy is it to take the common cup at Communion, when the person next you sneezes several times and gives a good deep rasp and drinks deep and then hands it to you? Suddenly your theology is spinning in your head.

What happens if the person next to you after Communion says: 'You are the first person to share a cup since I became HIV-positive'? What would that do to your head?

All the words, all the adjectives that we might use, that Jesus cuts across at the well, are now so comfortable for us. This was a radical, unhygienic, unsafe, unpopular moment. Some of our misguided Christian brethren are trying to restore some of that radical nature, even if they have grasped the wrong part of the nettle. There is an issue there about passion, about commitment, about living our faith in the real world. Jesus did not build a tent and wait for others to come to him to share the gospel.

The commentators are quite clear: this woman went in the middle of the day so that she would meet no-one. For whatever reason, she did not want to meet others; if you needed to draw water, this was not the time to go. No-one in their right mind would be at that well in the heat of the day. For that poor woman, this was the moment to be alone. At the very moment she thought she was alone, she met Jesus.

The other thing about this story is its inclusiveness. John, in this story, is trying to roll in as many difficult bits as he can: the fact that it is a Samaritan, a woman, the fact that they were going to share a vessel. What he is saying is what was real in his time, and it is just as real for us today.

The divisions we find are very deep within us. I was brought up in the West of Scotland. There, the distinction between Roman Catholic and Protestant was, and for many still is, deep. It is an inclusiveness that strikes at the very heart of what we are being told is acceptable. What comes to mind now when we hear the word Islam, what comes to mind when we hear the word Iraq or Palestine? Building the walls is much easier than knocking them down.

This is a radical moment of inclusiveness, not an interesting, ancient tale. Yet this story goes beyond the merely symbolic. It is a radical moment of Jesus doing something that is unacceptable, unhealthy, unclean, not really admired. He is acting with an inclusiveness that did not match the world. It is an earthly moment. Jesus talks about living water, using this as the opportunity to say that this is more than just a physical thirst. However, when he tried to do that, he found it difficult to communicate with the woman. She says, in a moment of crass misunderstanding 'give me this living water and it will save me coming back'. Just buy a little more at Tesco, 'buy one, get one free', and it will save me coming back. This is not what Jesus is saying. Jesus uses this radical, inclusive moment to say something about what our real deep needs are. They are more than physical, however we satisfy all these physical needs.

Watching Channel 4 last night, I realised we have a new Ten Commandments. You probably think they need updating. To 'what would your Ten Commandments be?' 40,000 Channel 4 viewers responded with theirs. For a second, I was taken back to the well, because these modern Ten Commandments will, when you hear them, seem very sensible, very caring and perhaps just where we are. As Jon Snow did last night, I list them in reverse order:

10   Protect your families

9   Never be violent

8   Look after the vulnerable

7   Protect the environment

6   Protect and nurture children

5   Do not steal

4   Be honest

3   Do not kill

2   Take responsibility

1   Treat others as you would have them treat you.

We are not going to argue with any of these. If we asked more people, then perhaps they would be in a different order. However, few of us would argue with any of them. You could hear people's minds clicking on the ones that have gone. Adultery has gone; for many people, it is no longer an issue.

These are all earthly moments, they are important, but there is not one mention of God. These are non-religious commandments. It begs the question, who will enforce them, but they are all earthly moments. There is no mention of graven images, no mention of the Sabbath and keeping it holy, no mention of having no other gods to command all our worship and all our attention apart from the one true God.

Religion has gone out of the Commandments. They are sensible, they reflect where we are. The first Ten Commandments, of course, were not done through a questionnaire among the Jews. These new ones are where we are, and you can see people's fears, anxieties, hopes and interests. So they talk about the environment, talk about children, talk about violence, talk about being honest, not to kill, taking responsibility, the way we treat others. Now you need to go back through the newspapers of the last two years. They will all appear, in the abuse of children, in the violence that goes on in our society, in how dishonest people can be and how it corrupts the lives of others, in the abuse of Iraqi prisoners. Treat others how you would like to be treated yourself.

We are not arguing with these; but these are earthly moments where God does not appear. It is the woman at the well. What Jesus is saying is that:

- this is about more than just simply supplying, or meeting, our physical needs,
- this is more than just a good ethical order of society,
- this is what you really need,
- this is deep within you.

Jesus is telling us: if all of these things were true, there would still be a longing, there would still be a need to be wanted and loved. There would be a need for a purpose in our world and a deep need to know that the world as we see it is not the final answer. Those whom we have loved and lost are not lost forever, and what we do here is part of a plan.

However difficult it is for us to understand, he is telling us that the living water which we crave is more than a symbol of physical thirst. It is a thirst for the knowledge of God in our lives. Furthermore, if we do not try to meet that need in others, if we do not try to share that need with others, they will compile their own commandments, where God is absent and they see no need for a living water that speaks beyond our earthly moments.

Jesus said to the woman: 'I come with living water, and with this you will thirst no more'.

Amen.

Sermon 15

Fear, Faith and First Steps

7 August 2004

Matthew 14:22–33

I returned from our holiday in France late on Thursday evening. We came through the tunnel. I am a tunnel man. I prayed for it, I gave thanks when it was opened and was disappointed when I did not have the funds to buy shares. I am a tunnel man because I am terrified of water. I get sick in a deep bath. I can understand the fear connected with water. Today's story is a very familiar one – Jesus walking on the water. It appears in three gospels, but Matthew's gospel is the only one to include the bit about Peter trying to copy Jesus. Peter tries to walk on the water. This is a story about fear, about faith and about taking the first step.

What are *you* afraid of? Someone I know very well is terrified of spiders. I have never been happy with heights, but it is not that sort of fear of which I am speaking. It is the kind of fear that can really grip us, that can paralyse us, that can make it difficult for us to think or to act or to move. Fear of change, failure, loneliness, death or meaninglessness. What makes us afraid as a church? When I went to write that list out, it was remarkably similar. Change, failure, apathy, death, opposition, ridicule? I can cope with my fear of water and heights because I do my best to avoid them. However, these other fears can

100

be deep-rooted and paralysing for individuals, as well as for churches, and we know people for whom they have ultimately become destructive forces. This is a story about fear, about faith and about taking that first step.

Peter shows a moment of discernment by making sure that it was Jesus who was there. Secure in the boat, the fishermen on the lake are in familiar territory when they see Jesus coming towards them; but, looking out from the security of their boat, they see something that makes them afraid. In many ways, they are quite happy to remain in the security of the boat. Peter, of course, is forever curious. Jesus speaks to them. Peter says: 'If it is you, them I am prepared to take the first step. If it is you, then I will come out of the boat and across to you.' In that sense, Peter showed commendable discernment before taking that first step.

There is much that calls us out of the security of whatever boat we are in, however fearful we are. Some of these calls will take our children from the boat we have created for them. When the command is spoken, Peter gets out of the boat – and, in that moment of faith, the faith is only real when it is married with the obedience. Peter's faith that it was Jesus would have meant nothing if he had remained in the boat; but he took the first step. So, it is a story about fear, about faith and about the first step.

I thought that was neat; but as is often the case, the gospel confounds the boxes we create. Peter was fearful, but then he has the courage of faith when he knows that it is Jesus, and he has the courage to take the first step – and what happens? He is fearful again. Suddenly, the boxes I tried to create were not quite so neat. Suddenly, I realised that, for Peter, having the faith to take the first step did not remove the fear. Overwhelmed by the magnitude of what he had done, at the scale of what was before him, when that first flush of faith and enthusiasm went and he suddenly realised what he had done, then he begins to sink.

ʿ Perhaps it is telling us that that first step of faith is not a step into a world where there is still no fear or worry. What is it, then? Jesus stretches out his hand and lifts Peter back into the boat. It is not a world that is absent of fear, but it is a world that is not absent of Christ. You can almost see Jesus with a wry smile, putting Peter back whence he came, perhaps commending him for his faith, or lack of it, but at least, he took the step. We have to understand the circumstances that put Peter in the water in the first place. He was not some sceptic saying 'I wonder if I will give this a go – I am not really sure' and taking a step out of the boat and sinking, saying 'I told you'. It was someone taking the step of faith. He becomes overwhelmed by the circumstances, and Jesus lifts him. It is a story about fear, about faith and about taking that first step.

If we identify what makes us fearful as individuals, or as a church, and if, individually and collectively, we pray for the faith that might help us take that step that may take us out of what makes us fearful, then we are assured not of a life void of future fear, but of a life in the presence of Christ who is there to lift us. When the fear returns, as inevitably it will, are we prepared to take the step out of the boat? Out of that which makes us comfortable, proud, arrogant, conceited? Out of that which presents us with no challenge, with no change, and to engage with what is beyond the boat?

Many psychiatrists and psychologists, in trying to identify why we have fear and anxiety, and what are the causes of fear and anxiety in the world, have identified three things which they see are at the root of much human anxiety and fear.

The first, they say, is *meaninglessness*, the idea that the world has no purpose, it is here by accident, that in a sense we are stumbling in the dark, we are victims of fate, we can do our best to muddle through, but ultimately this is meaningless.

The second thing they identify is *guilt*, both individual and corporate, a feeling of guilt for things we have said and done, the feeling of guilt for things we did not say when we should have. Things we did not do, when we should have acted. The guilt that many churches still have of realising that they are still not out of the boat. That only here within the security of the church can they affirm their faith, not out there, not in the heat of the kitchen, where their faith will not stand the test. There is often international guilt, the inability to solve the world's problems, when we know we could and we should. We can land on the moon, but we can not take food a few thousand miles. The guilt that acknowledges that the harvest of the world never fails, only our failure to share it. Meaninglessness and guilt.

The third thing that they have identified and that people have identified throughout the centuries is *death*. We do not talk about death, because it makes us fearful, either our own death, or the death of those who are close to us and whom we love.

Meaninglessness, guilt and death. So, what has the Christian faith to offer? What encouragement do we have to try and overcome our fear, to restore our faith and to take that first step?

What I wanted to use was a quotation which we often only use at funerals, and the problem is then that certain passages of Scripture and certain hymns become inevitably locked into these times. We rarely use them at other times. Jesus said: 'Set your troubled hearts at rest. Trust in God. Trust also in me. For in my Father's house there are many mansions.'

Just unpick that for a moment. If they are right, then one of the great sources of fear and anxiety among many people, even young people who cannot articulate it in that way, is *meaninglessness*. Jesus said: 'You believe in God', so believe in a God who created the world, who created it for a purpose and who has not abandoned it'. This is not about faith, about making do, but about a world that God saw and said was good and can be good again. You do not have to succumb to the meaninglessness and the fate that the world would have us believe.

Jesus also said: 'Believe in God and also in me', for he came to take on the sins of the world, that, however real *guilt* might be, either individually or collectively, if we turn and receive his pardon, we can be forgiven. We can wipe the slate clean, we can learn from the mistakes we have made and, through the power of his forgiveness, we can start again. How often we see, with some of the great figures of the past, how guilt has haunted them throughout their years and ultimately destroyed them. Jesus said: 'Come to me all who are weary and heavy-laden and I will give you rest'. He said to the thief on the cross: 'Today you will be with me in paradise'. We recognise the guilt, and we turn and receive his forgiveness, and we move on and we step out.

'Believe in God, believe also in me' – and Jesus said: 'For in my Father's house there are many mansions'. *Death* is not the end, but a new beginning, in a dimension which we are yet to experience. One of the great privileges of ministry is often to be with people who are ill and especially people whose life is drawing to a close. It has been one of my privileges here to sit with an elder of this congregation approaching death holding her hand in that hospital bed, and seeing, as well as the fear, the faith that will soon allow her to take the step out of the boat of life, knowing that here is a hand greater than mine to sustain her.

'Believe in God, believe also in me, for in my Father's house there are many mansions.' So, we take the first step, I hope. When I thought about taking the first step, I recalled my children's first step. I saw it. They were desperate to walk. Children want to take that first step. There is inbuilt in children an adventurous nature that wants to explore. If you have had children, you will know that whatever boat you build, they want out of it. We lose that when we grow up and become cynical, and so perhaps we have to restore some of the childlike curiosity and wonder and awe. Perhaps that is why Jesus said you must become childlike, adventurous and desperate to take that step, never happy with the boat you are in. So often, however much we have endeavoured to do things, the difference came with the step. Columba could have sailed for forty years, but it is when he stepped from the boat that things happened.

The Pilgrim Fathers could have sailed and sailed for years, but the United States of America began when they took the first step. We have just passed the anniversary of stepping onto the moon. We could circle the moon forever, but the moment we remember is when Neil Armstrong said: 'One small step for man; one giant leap for mankind'.

That wonderful moment with Peter in the boat is an encouragement to us all. We know by faith that it is Jesus himself who is calling us. 'If it is you, Jesus, then ask me to come to you.' Jesus replies: 'Come out of the boat'. Peter does, and he is overwhelmed, and he begins to sink, and Jesus lifts him. The story of Peter and Jesus on the water is the story of the disciples of every generation and the story of St Columba's. It is a story of fear and faith, and taking that first step.

Amen.

True Wisdom: The Skill to Listen

20 August 2006

1 Kings 2:10–12, 3:3–14

L ast Sunday, I conducted the service in St Andrew's Church of Scotland in Newcastle. Many will know that St Andrew's is linked with this congregation, and I preach there three times a year. I recall the first occasion I preached at Newcastle. The congregation there is very small, with only about forty attending. The church is small, the fellowship is warm, and, at the end of my first service, an elderly lady who had been a member at Newcastle for over seventy years shook me warmly by the hand and said to me: 'Lovely message, pet'. I read yesterday, she will not be allowed to say that any more. Newcastle Council has abolished using the word 'pet' because they say it is sexist and demeaning. This lady, thankfully, is no longer with us to read that nonsense. I was going to say she is probably turning in her grave; but, of course, as Christians, we believe she is not there. 'Lovely message, pet' will not be heard again apparently.

I flicked to the next page of my newspaper, hoping to read something a little wiser, and what did I discover? The owners of a funfair wanted to set up in Covent Garden, and the funfair has these little cars for the children to ride on. The owner of the funfair received a letter from Westminster City Council to say that, every day they turn it on, each of the cars will pay the £8 congestion charge. When someone approached Westminster City Council, they said it was a mistake and they should not have got that letter.

On the front page of that same newspaper were the exam results, with all the joys and sorrows that they brings. There were pictures on the front of the brightest kids and the youngest one and the oldest one, with all their achievements. It is a sad fact of life that, in the next few weeks, there will appear in the newspapers stories of those who could not cope with not getting what they wanted. In one newspaper, I read of someone recalling a wonderful old collect, an ancient prayer of the Church, praying that we may grow in wisdom as well as knowledge.

Our reading from the Old Testament today is one of the great readings of the Bible. Those of you who have been here over the past few weeks will know that the Old Testament readings follow the story of King David and the various exploits of that wonderful man. Now we read that David is dead and his son Solomon is to be king. In a dream, God says to Solomon: 'Ask for whatever you want and I will give it to you'. In that wonderful moment, Solomon says: 'I pray for a discerning heart to rule my people wisely and with justice, and to see the difference between right and wrong'. The gift of a discerning heart.

I want to reflect about the answer Solomon got, before we think about the answer he gave. God is pleased with Solomon, not just because of what he said, but because of what he did not ask for. Perhaps the Hebrew wisdom is telling us that many in our own day seek other things. God was pleased with Solomon because he did not ask for personal wealth or long life, nor did he ask for the death of his enemies.

Therefore, I would suggest that lurking in the hearts of all of us, and in that I include the pulpit, is a desire for these things, if we were able to have them. Often driven by the best possible motives, who would not wish for a long life, who would rejoice in any way about the deaths of children or young people, those cut down in untimely fashion with thoughts and prayers and things unfulfilled, with hopes diminished, with plans unrealised? It is part of the culture we now live in that we expect a long life, and if someone does not reach that long life, then somebody must be to blame, for long life is what we want.

Which one of us has not watched the lottery balls going round and has convinced ourselves of the wonderful things we would do with the £8 million:

- we would not spoil ourselves,
- it would not change us,
- we would still go to work.

'God, make my lottery numbers come up because as a Christian I will do the most wonderful things with this money.' Which one of us does not think perhaps in slightly less ambitious ways of just a little bit more, and all we could do with it? Who of us, in a moment of real honesty and heart-searching, when we look out on the iniquities and the evil in our world, does not seek the death of our enemies? We can ask for it without any vindictive feelings, but simply to put an end to the suffering they are causing others. It is like using the lottery for other people's benefit. The means might be slightly dodgy, but the end surely justifies the means.

God is pleased with Solomon's answer, but he is equally, if not pleased more, with the things he avoided asking for. This Hebrew wisdom goes to the very heart of our human nature. Why mention any of these things, why not simply say: 'Solomon, you have chosen well. I am pleased with you wanting a discerning heart'? It goes to the very heart of our humanity. 'I am also pleased you did not ask for those things that can so easily in their own form consume all of us and therefore can build up resentment when we do not get them – for long life, for riches and for the death of our enemies'. But Solomon asked for none of these things. He asked for a discerning heart.

Many will know that we are faced in the Church with a bewildering number of translations of the Bible. Many, I know, look back with great fondness to the Authorised Version and look with some bewilderment at all the editions we have had since. Every now and again, someone reflecting on passages can come up with a different translation that says something very deep to us. In this case, it is the New English Bible that has the most arresting version of 2 Kings 3. It reads: *Solomon says to God 'Give me a heart with the skill to listen'.* It is a wonderful translation. It reminds us that, for the Hebrew mind, wisdom is not something of the intellect.

I wonder if you know anyone who is wise? If I stopped for a moment and asked you to write down the names of people you knew who were wise, I suspect you would recall people who had perhaps not just intellectual ability but a good deal of common sense, the ability to see to the very heart of problems, to make clear and decisive decisions, to be able to see through the myriad options. While the Bible says a good deal about wisdom, it mentions none of these.

In our very cerebral world, where we are consumed by our intellectual achievements and our intellectual possibilities, this reading reminds us of the Hebrew mind, which sees wisdom not as an activity of the mind but as a direction of the heart. Wisdom in the Old Testament is always seen as something moral and ethical. Wisdom is seen as saying something about our relationship with other people and also our relationship with God. *The fear of the Lord is the beginning of wisdom* (Psalm 111:10) – and, in a world where we rightly would like more common sense, clearer thinking and, more decisive decisions, we also need to listen.

The story of the people in the Old Testament and in the New Testament tells us something about what this listening is. The first thing I would like to suggest is that it involves listening to ourselves. By that I mean the sense of being attuned to who we are, the gifts we have been given, the place God has for us in his purpose in the world. We have a heart to listen to ourselves, to have respect for ourselves, to recognise that we are part of God's purpose and part of his creation. Without the ability to attune our minds to whom we are and what we have, as well as what we would like to be, it would be difficult to listen to others. If we want an example of that, then we look at Jesus Christ himself. Jesus regularly took the time to be apart and to pray, to examine himself, to look inwardly, to recognise the mission and the purpose he had been given, to listen to himself. We pray for God's wisdom, a heart with the skill to listen, and that will include listening to ourselves.

However, it also includes listening to others. Have you ever spoken to someone who looks over your shoulder as you are speaking to them? If there is anything that induces possible violence, it is that. You are speaking to them, but they are clearly not listening. The ability to listen to others is more than simply hearing what they are saying. It is an ability to put yourself where they are, what we call empathy. Is there anything worse than the teacher who loses that ability to listen to his or her pupils? Is there anything worse for young people than to feel they are simply being lectured to? Is there anything worse than going to a doctor who you feel has absolutely no time to listen to you? You know what I mean: you are barely finished the sentence than the prescription pad is out? Is there anything worse for the congregation than feeling they are being harangued from the pulpit about all their sins from someone who has never really listened to their pain as well as their joy?

A heart with a skill to listen characterised the ministry of Jesus Christ. That is what set him apart from all the other famous teachers they had heard. Suddenly, they experience someone who was really listening to them. A teacher who got to the very heart of who they were, had a genuine sympathy and empathy, and wanted to understand. Jesus' replies to people in his ministry were always very appropriate for the person he was speaking to:

- whether it was the rich young ruler and his attachment to his wealth,
- whether it was someone who was sick
- or someone who had lost someone close to them.

Here was someone who really listened. He put himself where we are, so that he might help them. O, how we need wisdom, wisdom with a heart with the skill to

- listen to ourselves
- also to listen to others
- most of all to attune our hearts and minds to listen to God
- to really hear what God is saying to us
- wisdom to see these opportunities of worship as a moment not to step aside from the world but to receive God's Word and the courage to return to the world.

We have to take all our cleverness and all our intellectual powers, but also our wisdom, attuning our hearts to the will of God, and take that into a world that needs it most. That will be hard. Time and time again, when we listen for the Word of God, it seems to run counter to what we hear in the world. It seems to place us forever in a position of conflict with those who would present the world from their perspective. People who would tell us who is important and who is not. People who would tell us the people we can trust and the ones we cannot. Other religious people who will tell us who is in God's kingdom and who is beyond its bounds. People who will tell us what is right and wrong and just in the world. The power of communication now is such that everything we hear about the Middle East comes to us from our media and our politicians, so we had better be sure we can trust them.

Everything comes to us second or third hand. To that we must take the wisdom of God. Perhaps it is here, in moments of quiet, of prayer and of song, that we might have the ability to attune our hearts to what God is saying. However, before we leave this place, we need to ask for the courage to take it beyond these four walls and to take it into the world.

We look out on our world now and we are consumed with the problems of the Middle East. We are encouraging people to put aside old prejudice and old enmities and, when listening to others, try to put themselves in their place, not forever standing on their own. We look at the Holy Land, the land of the birth of our Lord, and we seek for all people in that land the wisdom that gives them a heart that can listen to themselves, listen to others, and ultimately listen to what God is saying. It will be part of our service and part of our prayers as individuals that we will pray for an end to hostilities. We will pray for help for those who are ill and injured and homeless and hungry. We will pray for a start for people getting together, but I suspect that all of it will count as nothing unless we also seek wisdom.

Amen.

Sermon 17

Agony and Ecstasy

6 March 2003

Mark 1:9–15

That most brilliant of political cartoonists, Brooks in *The Times*, was at it again this week. The cartoon on Tuesday depicts a courtroom. The judge is present with Gordon Brown, the Chancellor, holding a copy of a book which purports to be part of the Conservative party new ideas. Gordon Brown is arguing a case that all his best ideas have been stolen from him to complete this book. Opposite him, David Cameron, the leader of the Conservative party responds to the allegation, suggesting that he had managed to sell them, unlike the Chancellor. The cartoon was clearly an allusion to the case before the justices concerning the copyright of 'the Da Vinci Code', that most awful of books that has made a fortune. If I had written it and someone else pinched it, I would have kept quiet. However, as we all know, of course, money is involved.

It struck me, looking at the readings from last Sunday and this Sunday as we go into this season of Lent, that there is no other mainline faith that will ever take us to court for pinching the idea. They may debate that there are great similarities between Christianity and their own faith, in terms of ethical code, in terms of the importance of the Holy Book; in terms of people who are great prophets and exponents of the faith, in terms of the brave and courageous lives of those who followed that particular faith; but they will never take us to court for copyright over Lent, Holy Week and Easter, because suffering plays no part, other than in Christianity.

In some respects, we have to go back before we go forward. Last Sunday was Transfiguration Sunday, and I was preaching in Newcastle. My mother thinks that the Lord took me to Newcastle so that I would not gloat over Murrayfield in your presence. I did remind her that Newcastle was arranged a long time ago.

I have two books in my library – well, I have more than two books – but I have two particular books and they help ministers in the liturgical year, in planning services. One book concerns Advent, Christmas and the Epiphany, and the other concerns Lent, Holy Week and Easter. The one covering Epiphany finishes on the Sunday before Transfiguration Sunday, and the other one starts today. I wonder if someone was trying to tell us something about Transfiguration Sunday. Is it best just to ignore it? Yet Transfiguration Sunday is crucial for us as Christian people. It is odd that no-one mentions it, because it is a little difficulty set in between those great themes of the Christian year, Christmas and Easter. It acts as the hinge between the two.

The words uttered on the Mount of Transfiguration mirror and differ from the words uttered at Jesus' baptism. However, to do justice to that, we have to go back before we go forward, and I want to mention a reading that is actually the reading for next Sunday, but we need to put it back in the order in which Mark includes it.

With Jesus and the disciples, everything seems to be going well. They are not pleasing everyone, but there is great teaching. There is healing. People are flocking to Jesus. On the whole, all is going well.

In the passage that we will share in more detail next Sunday, which comes before the Transfiguration, Jesus says to his disciples: 'Now I need to tell you this: the Son of Man must suffer and must die'. Peter cannot cope with this. This is too much for Peter. How can this possibly be the end of this great rollercoaster of faith and emotion? So, when he says to Jesus that 'Somehow, suffering, your suffering is not part of this deal. That is not what we have signed up for', Jesus calls Peter 'Satan'.

Now, I do not know if anyone has called you 'Satan' before. I have had it twice, and on neither occasion could it be construed as a compliment. What is Jesus saying to his beloved disciple? He does not say to him: 'No Peter, you have missed the point; suffering is part of it, just bear with me'. Jesus calls him 'Satan'. There is no other moment of anger equivalent to that – perhaps even upturning the tables of the money-changers in the temple. In other words, Peter's inability to see that somehow suffering was part of this journey of faith provoked Jesus to call one of his most loved disciples 'Satan'.

The passage that follows is the Story of Transfiguration. There we are confronted with an account of this mystical experience of the disciples. During an experience that they find difficult to put into words, they hear a voice and it says: 'This is my beloved Son, listen to him'. Today the words said are addressed to Jesus: 'You are my beloved Son in whom I am well pleased'. What happened at Jesus' baptism, the confirmation that he was the Son of God, is now directed to the disciples.

Following Peter's inability to see that suffering is part of the journey of faith, the baptismal words are now addressed to Peter. 'This is still my beloved Son. What he has said to you about suffering does not make him any less my Son. The whole concept of suffering does not negate your faith. It does not unpick all the good things that we have done to this point. When I said, "You are my beloved Son in whom I am well pleased", I am now addressing it to you. This is still my beloved Son, listen to him.'

Peter, in that moment on the Mountain of Transfiguration, wants to hold onto that moment forever. He wants to build the shelters on that mountain, and he wants to stay in that high moment of Christian ecstasy. However, down the mountain they must come and begin that journey to Jerusalem.

Today, Mark wants to put the two together. In the other accounts, in Matthew and Luke, we have longer accounts of the temptation. You will remember Jesus being tempted to turn stones into bread, and throw himself from the top of the temple and have power over all the kingdoms of the world. Mark, in a sense, is not concerned with the detail but simply with the juxtaposition of baptism and temptation and it is exactly the same the other way around – of Peter denying that suffering has any part in the experience of the Mount of Transfiguration.

They are both reminders, at the beginning of this Lenten journey, of the agony and the ecstasy that belong to the Christian journey. They remind us that they both play their part; and it is not right to have one without the other. It is interesting on these two Sundays that the agony and the ecstasy are reversed; Peter denies the suffering and then experiences the Mount of Transfiguration. Today, Jesus experiences the high point of his baptism and the confirmation he is God's Son, but it does not lead to a little 'do' in Bethany. It does not lead to a little cheese and wine chez John. Instead, it leads him to the desert and to temptation.

I think it is a reminder to us all as we begin this Lenten journey that that is the Christian life. It is part of our human nature that we would all love to stay on the mountain-top. We would all love to experience that high moment of Christian faith and assurance and not be troubled about what awaits us at the bottom of the mountain. The significance of this Lenten journey is not just that Christ came, but that he came and stood where we stand – tempted as we are, but without sin.

The season of Lent is a preparation. It began with the early Church as a preparation for their baptism. This was a time of self-examination, of examining the faith and all that it meant to follow Jesus. It culminated after forty days of this study with baptism on Easter Eve, joining the community of faith in that struggle.

What I have just said is glaringly obvious, of course, to us all. We know how difficult the Christian life is. We know how hard it is to take any of the high points of our faith in worship, in song, in prayer, in reading back into that world that awaits us. We are often not faced with the great moral dilemmas of what is good and what is evil, but we are tempted, as Jesus was tempted, with those very seductive options – the ones that seem superficially attractive.

In the account in Luke's gospel, the devil says to Jesus: 'Why do you not turn these stones into bread?' Well, what is wrong with that? Is not that why he came? Would not that, in a spiritual sense, or even in a physical sense, be the reason that Jesus came? Let us cut to the chase, let us cut out the years of anguish in between; there is no need for the Cross. He has the opportunity to do something wonderful for the world. However, Jesus says: 'No'.

'Throw yourself from the top of this temple and your angels will save you. Surely that kind of stunt will convince everybody that you are the Son of God and they will be faithful. Is not that why you came? Would not that solve all your problems about bringing people to faith? In the face of that, how could they not follow you?' Then Jesus said: 'No'.

The devil showed him all the kingdoms of the world and said: 'If you would only worship me, then all these kingdoms would be yours. Is not that why Jesus came – to win the kingdoms of the world and make them the kingdom of God?' Yet Jesus said: 'No. The end does not justify the means.'

Today begins our Lenten journey. The hard journey that leads to the Cross and beyond. It is another reminder that perhaps we are moving away from the ecstasy of Christ's ministry to the agony of this journey and the Cross and beyond. However, they are all part of the life to which we will now return. We see the face of Jesus when we look back on our lives at time of tension and difficulty, or in times of illness and bereavement. On occasions, we have wondered how we could possibly cope with what life has dealt us – and yet we have coped. When we look back, we realise that, for that moment, we have seen the transfigured Christ leading us forward. We know that there will be testing times ahead.

These Sundays at the beginning of this journey remind us that, when these times come, they do not negate our faith, and when we bring our agony and our tears and our doubts before God, we are somehow not less of a Christian than we were last week. Jesus, when he heard, his friend Lazarus had died, wept as we weep when those close to us die. He reflected what is our experience so often. When he went to the Cross, he recognised that death is part of our life, and he hung there for us and he rose again for us to remind us that it is not the end.

We go on this Lenten journey knowing that we journey not alone, and we recognise that none of the other great faiths will take us to court for copyright, for pinching their idea; but it is the life of Christ; and it is the great hope that we offer to the world.

Amen.

Nature of the Church

The Pivotal Point of the Gospel

2 April 2006

St John 12:20–33

I was on the Internet during this past week booking a hotel room. This particular hotel e-mailed me back to say: 'We have a reservation; we have a room available. All you need to do is to send a photocopy of both sides of your credit card.' It filled me with some horror; the hotel is in sub-Saharan Africa. So, I was looking for the usual encrypted messages – I decided not to do it.

Credit-card fraud is one of the biggest areas of fraud, and runs into billions. So, you can imagine how pleased I was when I read in yesterday's *Times* that they were trying to tighten the security with our credit cards. Perhaps you recognise now that from 14 February the great thing is 'Chip and PIN'.

In yesterday's *Times*, technology is moving on. Now it is going to be 'Chip and Sing'. It will soon be that British banks, and I quote, 'are developing security for credit cards using tonal range in the voice which is more secure than even someone else knowing your number'. The article said: 'Fraud has fallen since "Chip and PIN" was made compulsory, but people struggle to remember their numbers. The chief technician for the British Banking Federation said, "High-street transactions have been suffering, so we are looking at alternatives; till and cash machines will have microphones. The trouble is that if people struggle to recall their PIN there is always a chance they will forget which song they are meant to sing. So we need to have one song that everyone knows. We do not want some old lady belting out "My Way", when she should be singing from the "Halleluiah Chorus".[1]

Yesterday was 1 April and it became apparent that this was an April Fool courtesy of *The Times*. The end of the article gave it all away: 'This Lyrical Input Elocution System will be in by 2009'. 'Lyrical Input Elocution System' of course spells 'Lies'.

Today's story could have been written for April Fools' Day. The seductive charm of an April Fool is that people need to be drawn in. It cannot be so ridiculous that nobody will believe you from the minute you open your mouth. Something has to draw you in. For those of you who are old enough to remember the BBC telling us that spaghetti grew on trees, perhaps that was just a little bit too ridiculous. There needs to be a seductive part of the story; there needs to be something that draws people to listen to the story, and it is only as it unfolds that perhaps people recognise that it is an April Fool.

This really is for this Sunday, in particular, and for a big chunk of Lent, in general. This is a pivotal moment in John's gospel, as it is in the season of Lent. In chapters 1–10 John is telling us about the life and the teaching of Jesus. In the latter part of chapter 12 through to 20 is the story of his passion and his resurrection. At the beginning of John's gospel comes the well-known prologue, and at the end comes an epilogue in chapter 21. In between those great themes in John's gospel comes this story – the rather innocuous-looking story of the two Greeks who want to see Jesus. It is, however, a turning point in the story. I think, for the first hearers, it must have sounded a bit like an April Fool when Jesus explained what was going to happen.

On several occasions, Jesus says: 'The time is not right, my hour has not come'.

- He says it to his mother.
- He says it to the Samaritan woman.
- He avoids arrest because, time and time again, Jesus says: 'The time is not right, the hour has not come'.

So, I imagine that the disciples must have been wondering: 'Why the wait? What will trigger the right time?' Perhaps, during all of their time with Jesus so far, they thought: 'This will be the moment. This is a moment of great controversy with the authorities; this is the moment – the hour has come.' However, it passed. 'One of the great teachings; one of the great miracles: this is surely the moment, the hour has now come.' They were always the ones who thought they knew the right moment.

Now, at last, in John 12, Jesus says: 'The hour has come'. 'Great,' said the disciples, 'but what has caused it?'

- What has caused it is not one of the great miracles in the Bible;
- What has caused it is not one of the great controversies with the authorities;
- What has caused it was not a deeply meaningful spiritual moment with his disciples.

It is a few Greeks who say: 'We would like to see Jesus'.

Philip tells Andrew, and Andrew tells Jesus. It is a kind of 'bank-manager scene:' 'Sorry to bother you, Jesus, but there are some Greeks outside who want to see you'. In response, Jesus said: 'Now the hour has come'. That must have sounded a bit like an April Fool; what an anticlimax 'That cannot be; surely not now.' So, what was it about this story that prompted Jesus to say: 'Now is the hour'?

The rest of John's gospel unfolds after the stories in Bethany and Jesus being anointed; signs of his death; signs of new life and resurrection in Nazareth. This week finishes Lent; next week is Palm Sunday and we enter into the events of Holy Week. In the lead-up to this passage, there are two pivotal things that John sees as the themes for Jesus saying: 'Now is the time'. This passage actually follows the events of Palm Sunday when Jesus rejects any notion of a triumphal entry into Jerusalem to overthrow the authorities. Probably this was the expectation of most of the people at the time. So, in a very visual way, Jesus seems to humiliate himself while he destroys that view by riding in not on a military horse, a charger, but on a donkey.

The Greeks: non-Jews. The Gentile world wants to see Jesus. There is a note of universalism; suddenly there are non-Jews. Not the Jewish authorities; not the disciples, but that wide outside world of which we have heard so little. Now they want to see Jesus – and the word used for these Greeks clearly means that they were not Jews, nor even converts to Judaism. They were simply inquisitive Greeks of their time.

The Greeks loved a debate and an argument with the disciples, as we see from the Book of Acts. Perhaps they had heard of this Jesus, perhaps they had heard him preach, seen him perform miracles, and their curiosity drove them to say: 'We would like to see Jesus for ourselves'. It seems to be at that moment when Jesus recognises:

- there is a curiosity,
- there is a hunger,
- there is a thirst,
- not just among the Jews, but among the whole world.

Jesus says: 'Now is the moment for the Son of Man to be glorified'. When the authorities see the effect of the Palm

Sunday events they say with some exasperation, 'What can we do, for – look – the whole world is after him?' They say that as Jesus is riding on a donkey.

This idea of universalism is one that many Christians do not like; many Christians would rather see the heavenly places, the special places, the promises of God remain for the elect; they are only for the Christian few. They somehow do not like the idea that God's purpose is that the Lamb of God took away the sin of the whole world. There are some Christians who would say: 'Well, I will list for you a few for whom I think that that is unlikely',

It was when the Greeks came enquiring about Jesus that he said: 'The time has come'. He did it by riding into Jerusalem on a donkey. The universalism of the sacrifice of Jesus and the humility of those who followed him triggered the start of the journey to Jerusalem. Just in case they thought the entry to Jerusalem was back to their old thoughts, right at the end of our passage John says: 'Jesus told them this to tell them the kind of death he was going to die'. This has been the theme throughout Lent, starting with Transfiguration Sunday, introducing the idea of suffering and death into the story of Christian life.

You remember that everything was going fine with the disciples until Jesus said: 'I think the time is now right for the disciples to get the whole story'. Jesus tells Peter that he needs to suffer and to die, but Peter cannot cope with the idea that a life following Christ includes suffering. That was what prompted Jesus to call Peter 'Satan', not recognising that part of this journey involves suffering. From there, they moved to the Mount of Transfiguration, where the voice of God at his baptism, addressed to Jesus, is now addressed to the disciples: 'This is my beloved Son; this is still my beloved Son who is talking about suffering'.

Therefore, as this Lenten journey continues, the disciples are becoming more aware, in a way perhaps they cannot understand, that suffering is part of the human journey. It does not deny God's existence; it does not negate God's presence, for God in Christ has also suffered. Today is the turning point of that idea of suffering, not being self-destructive and self-pitying, for out of it comes something of beauty and of worth.

Then Jesus, for the benefit of his listeners, uses another agricultural analogy with which they would be familiar. He compares our life to a grain of wheat. He says: 'If there is something you keep in isolation, whether it is the seed or your own life, glorying in it for itself, divorced from your role in the world, in the same way as keeping a seed and staring at it, then that is not lifting up your cross and following me'.

Perhaps, just when the disciples were getting most depressed about this idea of suffering, comes the other side of the same coin. For out of that suffering, out of that Cross, comes Easter Day. Out of that death comes new life. Out of that self-sacrifice, comes a life devoted to others. For, unless a seed dies and is buried, there will be no new life. Unless Christ dies and rises again, there will be no resurrection. Unless we die in our own lives to sin, selfishness, arrogance and pride, we miss out on the chance of living that eternal life now.

The Greeks said to Philip: 'We would like to see Jesus' – and that acknowledgement, if not of faith, then was at least a thirst, a hunger, from the non-Jewish world to see Jesus for themselves. It prompted Jesus to say: 'Now is the hour'. We live in a world where that hunger still exists. For the Greeks, you could substitute anyone who is not in the Church. Do not think that those who have a hunger and a thirst for righteousness and spirituality are only those who are in the pew! There are millions of Greeks of our own day who are saying: 'We would like to see Jesus. We do not know what it will mean. We do not know what it will say to us. We do not know what difference it will make' – but they have made the first step.

They said to Philip: 'We would like to see Jesus' – and it is a reminder to the church that what we say, and what we do, as a church, must not prevent people from seeing Jesus for themselves. We do not ask people to come and marvel at our cleverness, or our pretensions, or to be thrilled by our traditions.

I hope that, if and when they do come, they will see the same humility in his people as they saw in Jesus when his glory was measured not by the measure of the world but by the ridiculous sight of him dragging his feet on the ground on the back of a small donkey.

There are Greeks saying to us now: 'We would like to see him' – and I hope they may see something of him in the humility of his people and the sacrificial nature of their life. When I say 'they', that means you and me.

Amen.

1. Alexi Harpor, *The Times*, London (1 April 2006) © NI Syndication, London (1 April 2006).

Sermon 19

Where Might God Be Found?

24 August 2003

1 Kings 8:1, 6. 10–11. 22–30, 41–3
John 6:56–69

It was nearly twenty-one years ago that I was inducted to my very first parish. I was full of enthusiasm! The task before us was a very easily identifiable one: we had to redecorate the church. It was in an awful state. It had not been painted for nearly seventy years. The sanctuary looked dowdy. We believed that it affected worship. Give it a lick of paint. To do it properly required closing the church. So, for three months we worshipped in the hall. On our first Sunday when we had moved out of the church, as the congregation gathered, one of my elders said to me: 'Leave the church door open, so that God will hear us'. The clear implication was that God was not in the hall. In his mind, somehow, God resided only in the sanctuary.

It is difficult to escape this perception. Perhaps an examination of our readings might help us to gain a different perspective. Our reading this morning from First Kings is about the dedication of the temple. The second reading, from John's gospel, concerns the body of Christ, the Word made flesh in person. I want us to look briefly at the First Kings reading as the hope and the John reading as the reality.

I

First of all, the hope. This was the moment that the people of Israel had been awaiting for so many years: the building and the dedication of the their beloved temple. This was not just a building to which some would occasionally go to worship. This was at the very heart of their life together. For many generations they had worshipped without such a building, but now the splendid temple had been built, and it required a proper dedication.

Dignitaries were invited. It was an important occasion. Here we have the record of King Solomon coming and standing before the Ark of the Covenant and offering a prayer. He offers a prayer for the temple, and he offers a prayer for the people. I want us to reflect briefly on three things in that prayer. It is a pivotal moment in Old Testament theology because of the scope and the breadth and the radical nature of that prayer.

What does Solomon say on that occasion? In the midst of that beautifully constructed temple, the first part of his prayer is a reminder to people that God is not restricted to that place. Never mind opening the doors so that God might hear us in the hall. In the midst of that temple, he is reminding the people that God is present everywhere in their lives and has been, whether it is the desert or whether is the newly dedicated temple. God cannot be contained in whatever we construct, however magnificent. All we build is but our feeble attempt to lift our hearts and minds to God. What a marvellous way to begin! This is the magnificent temple, built to the glory of God – but God is not confined to that place.

Then he goes on to say that the temple should be a place in which to offer our hearts and lives to God. Jesus' words when he overturned the temple money-changers' tables are the only time in the gospel records, or anywhere else, when we have a glimpse of the anger of Jesus. I have said before that there is no caring, sharing way to upturn the tables. He was furious.

Given the history of Israel, I refuse to believe that the temple was constructed without anyone falling out. I refuse to believe that, on that occasion, everyone had their hearts and minds turned to God. It was not true then, and it is not true this morning. The people of Israel were as fallible and as weak and as feeble as we are, yet they offered what they had as their best worship. Perhaps, in some minds, there was confusion that this beautiful, magnificent setting was somehow a symbol of some something else such as the institution's wealth, or its authority. How easy it is to take that gentle walk to the moral high ground!

The second thing that Solomon said was that it was a *house of prayer.* Did you notice that passing reference, in that wonderful reading, to what must be, for many people in the pew, their ultimate prayer? *'The spirit of God filled the people so much that the priest could not get on with their worship.'* What a marvellous picture! The spirit of God was so obviously evident in that place that even human attempts to worship failed! *This shall be a house of prayer.* Do not confuse it with anything else.

Do not ever underestimate the power of prayer, or the presence of God among his people. Standing there in that newly built temple is the hope, not only that generations will offer their hearts and minds to God, but that they will remember that God is not restricted to that place – and that place is the house of prayer.

Thirdly, we have words of encouragement. There are many incidents and circumstances in life when people will need God's sustaining presence. They more often than not occur when they are not in services of worship in a beautiful building of worship. Solomon finishes his prayer of dedication by saying that we do not leave God behind when we leave here. We will probably need him more when we are not here, when we are not in that sustaining presence of those who think like us, when we are not in that atmosphere of worship which can be very moving. What a way to finish the prayer!

Shortly, we will leave – and where will God be then? Solomon says, in this list of things, we will need God's presence as previous generations did in the desert, and then God will be there because we do not leave God behind in the sanctuary. This is the hope, surely not only of those ancient Jewish people, joyous and uplifted in their new temple, but the prayer of the Church throughout the generations as we sit in a beautiful building and worship God. That is the hope.

II

What then of the reality? The early Church had no buildings, no churches as we know them. They probably did not worship in the same place twice. Many of them were Jews and would return to the temple, but the early Christians were an itinerant people following the Word made flesh. What was the reality then?

So, we need to listen to the gospel of John as it addresses our situation. It is clear that it was not comfortable when it was recorded, or when it was first heard. We are told: 'This is hard teaching, and some disciples departed'. This is one of the most astonishing passages in John's gospel.

In the chapters in John's gospel preceding this, how is this for a list?

- Jesus changes water into wine
- he cleans the temple
- he talks to the Samaritan woman

131

- he heals the official's son
- he feeds the 5,000
- he walks on water

and they are still with him.

But now they say: 'This is hard teaching'. What is this hard teaching? It is Jesus saying: *'I am the bread of life'*. 'What your forefathers ate in the desert sustained them physically for a while, but they died, but whoever eats of this bread eats of me and will live forever.'

Having experienced all of that and stayed with him, this statement is too much. Why?

- What was it about this bit of the teaching what prompted some to fall away?
- Could it be that Jesus was speaking directly to them?
- Could it be that, for the first time, this was something that affected them physically and spiritually and emotionally?
- Was it suddenly that they had moved from being observers to being participants?

Jesus is inviting us, like the disciples, to see things from a new perspective. He is challenging us to hear his words as if they are addressed to our lives now. 'You have watched and you have listened and you have followed, but now is about you. Now it is about what will sustain you. It is about your response and your eternal life.' This is the hard teaching. So, what connects our two readings this morning? It is:

- How to make that hope a reality?
- How to make us move from being observers, in worship and in our witness, to being participants?
- How can we move from saying 'God is in this place' to realising that God might also be waiting in our hearts?

- How God might also want to change me, not just the person in front of me in the pew because I know the person sitting needs it more than I do?

But what about me? It is how to move from this idea of observing to participating. It is not easy in our Presbyterian worship when we are racked up in pews. It was not easy when there was no church building. They did not need to sit in a pew to feel as if they were observers. They followed Jesus, and they saw what he did, and suddenly he turned and said to them: 'Who do you say I am? This bread is for you.' Suddenly they were a little worried. This was hard teaching, and for some it was too much. The opportunity for us is to face up to the implication of what Jesus us saying and accept that we are being called to live in a new way.

We gather here in this beautiful building. We lift our hearts and minds to God, and we keep before us Solomon's prayer: *'God is not restricted to that which we build with our hands or in our minds'*. Whatever our thoughts are as we gather for worship, it is a house of prayer where we seek his forgiveness and we ask for his strength. God is not, however, restricted to this place. God will go with us. We do not leave God behind. How do we make that hope a reality? When we read, when we pray, when we sing. God is not speaking to the person next to you or to me – God is speaking to you and me, are we ready to hear what God is saying?

Amen.

Sermon 20

When What We Say Is What We Do

30 October 2005

Matthew 23:1–12

Practising what we preach

For those who want to take a few words of comfort this morning, Jesus' devastating words in Matthew's gospel seem to be about religious leaders. Preachers should be very careful preaching on these verses when we stand among you dressed like this. Oh, they loved to wear their robes, they loved to wear their long tassels, and they loved to put loads of responsibilities of guilt on others, but never seemed to carry them themselves. They loved the best seats at the banquet and enjoyed being greeted in the market place.

Today's reading is about hypocrisy. It is here in Matthew's gospel that we get that famous phrase so often used: 'Why do you not "practise what you preach?".' Nothing turns people away from the Church more than the gap between what we say and what we do. There is a sense in which that is even worse than not doing anything. It is building up a climate of expectation and then doing nothing, or doing something that undermines what we say. Nothing turns young people off the Church more than prim and proper middle-class people, well dressed, who like to sit in pews (and I am quoting from young people) and who can say and sing and pray the most marvellous things, but have you heard some of the things they say on the steps of the church on the way out?

This is nothing new. Practising what you preach is a reading we have read from the first century. Hypocrisy is nothing new, but the challenge has always been to bridge the gap between what we say and what we do. We must continue to practise what we preach. Before we say anything about that phrase, one thing we have to say is: 'What exactly do we preach, and why is there a gap?'

In the context of worship, and in the content of our hymns and prayers, we can say things that we deeply believe. We can say things about how we want to live our lives as Christian people, and we know what God requires of us. The reason that we do not often act this way is not simply because we are hypocritical. That is a cynical view that does not touch where people are. While it might be true of some, it is by no means the whole story for the people of God. Sometimes, we cannot practise what we preach because it is simply too hard. We live in a world that seems to be too hard for the gospel we have received; somehow we just do not have the energy.

During a recent visit to the USA, we stayed at Princeton, and we went to the theatre one night and saw a play entitled *Miss Witherspoon*. We saw it on the last performance before it went to New York, off Broadway. It is a play by one of America's brightest young talents, and it is a biting satire on modern life. Miss Witherspoon is in heaven, and when she gets to heaven she is greeted by an Indian lady in a sari and Miss Witherspoon finds this very difficult to cope with. Miss Witherspoon indicates that she was expecting St Peter, who would be elderly, white skinned and have a long beard. In fact, she was expecting a heaven shaped by her Christian heritage. The woman in the sari agrees that there is a Christian heaven, a Buddhist heaven, a Muslim heaven and a Jewish heaven. Miss Witherspoon is astonished at the idea of Jewish heaven, because, as far as she understands it, the Jews do not have any belief in an afterlife. The Indian lady confirms that this is right, but suggests that they are under something akin to a perpetual general anaesthetic.

It was a biting satire on what we believe and what we take into the world. It was a reminder that the Church cannot, and will not, survive on a medieval theology and a Victorian morality. That no longer serves us in the world that we are called to serve, which has more in keeping with the first century than it was with the nineteenth. It is all very well to say that we must match our actions to what we preach – but what do we preach? Do we know what we should preach? Sometimes we do not practise what we preach because we do not have the energy, or we do not have the theology, or we do not have the tools, necessary to meet the world that we are called to serve.

This is a church which takes seriously the book of Psalms and the book of Job with all the questions about the presence of God in the midst of evil and suffering. Part of the challenge of Christian people is, before we ever think about how we are going to act, to ask: 'What do we believe?' That is a lifelong struggle of the things of the faith. What we preach is Christ crucified and risen. When Paul wrote to the Thessalonians, he said: 'When we came to you, I was so glad that the word we gave you – you believed it, not as my word, but as it rightly is; the Word of God. We do not preach ourselves, but Christ crucified and risen. We do not preach ourselves, but the Christ who came and touched and healed and forgave all those from the margins of society – those whom others counted as nothing.'

In a few weeks' time, it will be the fifth anniversary of my induction to St Columba's. Before I came to St Columba's, I was in discussion and interview with various members of the Vacancy Committee. I will never forget one question I was asked by one member of the Vacancy Committee.

This struck me very deeply. 'If you came to London,' was the question, 'would you be prepared to visit someone and bury someone who had AIDS?' I knew, by the discussion I had had, that the question was being asked to make sure that I could say 'Yes'. Some congregations ask it to make sure the minister will say 'No'. Perhaps here was a congregation prepared to *say* and to *do* the same thing. To say on the one hand that God in Christ came to touch all those whom no-one else would touch is fine, but what about the practice?

Sometimes we do not practise what we preach. Not because we are hypocritical, but just because it is too hard. We live in a world that is telling us what is acceptable and what is not, and the gospel does not sit easily with it. It is telling us that there are nations which in themselves are evil, there are faiths other than Christianity which, in themselves, are evil. There are people of race, or colour, or creed, or sexual orientation, who have no place in the Church.

While it may be easy for many of us, as liberals, to say 'No, I do not quite see that. That is going too far', it can nonetheless paralyse us and prevent us from acting in the way we should. Practise what you preach. What is it that we preach? We preach Christ crucified and risen and all that that contains. Sometimes we do not do that. Not for reasons of hypocrisy, but because in the world in which we are set it is just too hard.

I looked up the meaning of the word 'hypocrisy' in the *Chambers Dictionary*. 'Hypocrisy' is defined there as, 'Acting or playing a part' – and that seems to fit well with Matthew's gospel. 'Feigning to be better than one is, or to be what one is not.' Then it says this: 'concealment of true character or belief, *not necessarily consciously*' – so, suddenly, the word, hypocrisy, draws all of us in. Do we practise what we preach? Often we do not. Not because we are cold and callous, not because we are hypocritical, pretending to be something we are not; often because it is sometimes just too hard to take the gospel to a world obsessed

- with achievement,
- with people being able to cope,
- with thinking there is an answer to everything even if we have not got it now,
- by the material things we amass,
- with size as an indicator of success.

One of the other churches in New York which Hilda and I visited on our first Sunday there is Fifth Avenue Presbyterian Church at East 55th Street. Some time ago, Fifth Avenue Church took the difficult decision to sue the Mayor of New York was because he was instructing the police to arrest homeless people who were sleeping on the steps of Fifth Avenue Presbyterian Church.

The Session at Fifth Avenue said: 'This is an issue about practising what we preach'. It is to say that homelessness is not a criminal offence. The Church won the case. They said: 'All the things that we say in this wonderfully historic church Sunday by Sunday would have been diminished if we had said nothing about the arrest of homeless people. We must practise what we preach.'

Hypocrisy in the sense in which it is used in Matthew's gospel is not simply a jibe to make those in the pew feel uncomfortable. It is a recognition that, first and foremost we must recognise what it is we preach, for that will determine the practice. We preach none other than Christ crucified and risen. If it is the gospel of Christ that we preach, then that directs our practice, so we ask for the faith and the courage to go from this place and to practise what we preach in a world which does not like it.

To have the energy and the resources to do that,

* Come now to the table.
* Come now and receive the body and blood of that crucified and risen Christ that we preach.
* Come, everyone, from all branches of the Christian Church.
* Come because you love the Lord Jesus a little and you would like to love him more.

Rosa Parks died this week. In the 1950s, she refused to give up her seat on the bus in Montgomery, Alabama, when a white male boarded the bus. Under the law, he had a right to the seat. Her courage led to the Civil Rights movements and a change in the law. The Presbyterian Church of the USA paid tribute to Rosa Parks on their official website. They consider that she practised what she and they preached.

One Sunday, a minister was delighted to see, sitting with her parents in the congregation, a girl who had become an unmarried mother at a very young age. She had caused all sorts of scandal and talk in the church, and, when it came time for the Sacrament, she passed the goblet to her mother, not taking it. The minister reflected afterwards: 'Just for a moment, I knew I had to do something. Sometimes you get these moments where the whole of your life flashes before you. Suddenly I realised: I need to practise what I preach.' So, he went down the steps, and he went to the mother, and, when she had finished, he took the goblet and then he gave it to the daughter and said: 'This is for you'.

Come now to the holy table; receive the Body and Blood of the one we preach for: that is what we should practise.

Amen.

New Year Resolutions
or New Year Encounters?

7 January 2007

Isaiah 43:1–7

I would like to take the opportunity to wish those whom I have not seen yet this morning a very happy New Year. What a dreary bunch we look. The church, and I suspect many of our homes, look as if we have just been robbed. The decorations are all gone, the tree is down, the tinsel and the glitter have gone. So much effort was put into our Christmas celebrations, but now they have disappeared. This Sunday seems in such contrast. It is back to work, back to school soon, back to old clothes and porridge. Oh, the joys of being Presbyterian!

It was compounded for me this morning at half past nine when I got a text message from my golfing friends in Florida. A trip I had to pull out of because of a knee injury. It just said: 'missing you'.

Last Sunday, we brought in the New Year in Scotland. For me, it was the first time in many years. Last Sunday morning, Hilda worshipped in the church in Ayr, having brought in the New Year with her mother. I worshipped in the parish church near our flat in Glasgow, having brought in the New Year with my mother. It is a church I know reasonably well, and they are nice folk.

It was an all-age service for the end of the year. The minister was talking about New Year resolutions. So, we had the usual:

- give up smoking,
- reduce the chocolate,
- try to go to bed the same day I get up – which, apparently, is not the same as getting up the same day you go to bed!

The minister wanted to try to move on from this and tried to say: 'What about resolutions as a church?' He then referred to the previous year, and said: 'I noted down the resolutions that we made as a congregation last year just to see how well we are doing'.

Then he asked: 'What about new ones, what about New Year resolutions for the church?' 'We need better signs', somebody said. Someone else said: 'But the paper gets damp'. So someone else said: 'I promise to laminate them', and I said to myself: 'Lord, take me now'. That was where these good folk had got to. Their resolution for the New Year for the church: better laminated signs.

The minister was trying very courageously to rescue a dying cause, and he said: 'I want to make a resolution for the church. My resolution for the church is that every visitor to this church in the coming year will have a conversation with at least three people before they leave the church. "Good morning" at the door does not qualify as a conversation.' Not being the shy retiring violet type, as you know, I had three failed attempts to engage people in conversation. I know, outside the door, they are lovely folk; but laminated signs are their goal.

So, here we are as a congregation standing on the cusp of a new year. Do we make any resolutions as a congregation or as individuals? I mean real ones, resolutions that truly matter? Are we resolving to do or to say something, or to refrain from doing or saying something that will matter and that will really cost us and that will really make a difference?

Today is the Orthodox Christmas. It seems a shame to take down the tree. I was brought up in the Cathedral in Glasgow, where the tree will be up for another couple of weeks – the full Christmas season. We would still be singing Christmas carols even though today is the Sunday after the Epiphany.

Traditionally, the Epiphany has been associated with the wise men. The word 'epiphany' means 'the manifestation', 'the showing of' the glory of Christ to the Gentiles, represented by the wise men. Yet, today's reading, traditionally on the first Sunday after the Epiphany, concerns the baptism of Jesus. In a way, it is also an epiphany. It is the showing, the manifestation, that this *is* the Son of God when he comes and is baptised by John.

The Christmas stories and the manifestations are all about encounters. As far as we know, Jesus

- wrote no books,
- organised no conferences,
- compiled no pamphlets,
- conducted no seminars.

Yet, the gospel story is a story of encounters. This is a reminder that the Incarnation and the gospel of Christ is about our relationship with people, and there is no substitute for that.

The written Scriptures and the theology all came after people encountered God in Christ. If we have any task as a church, it is to help others and to help ourselves to have this encounter. We are expected to participate in the manifestation of the light of God through our own lives because we live increasingly in a world which is more impersonal. In a computerised mechanised world, personal encounters are at a premium.

I remember, just after 11 September 2001, attending a vigil service at Westminster Abbey which the recently retired Dean, Dr Wesley Carr, had organised. In that service, he gave a very moving and touching three-minute address on the theme of the mobile phone. What started out as a fashion accessory became a method of communication between loved ones for the final time from those aircraft. Now mobile phones record the hanging of Saddam Hussein. If that tells us anything, it is that technology is neutral.

I used to have a very old poster, one of the first computer posters, which simply said: 'Garbage in, Garbage out'. Whatever comes out of a computer is what some human being, however intelligent, has put in. However, we live in a world where we can demonise technology. We can condemn sensationalism on television and the press, but it is about people:

- how people use their mobile phones,
- how people use or abuse the Internet,
- how creative or destructive people are in all the media that we use and enjoy and rely upon so much.

Now, some people think that the more sophisticated the world gets, the less relevant the Christian faith is. I would argue the opposite. The Christian faith's unique contribution to the world is this encounter between God and his people. And there is no parallel in any other faith. When we sing 'See in yonder manger low', we are asserting that God has come 'down to such a world as this'.

It is about encountering God in Christ and the gospel story that will now begin to unfold yet again.

- It is about Jesus encountering people, not espousing theology.

- It is about Jesus meeting people at the most vulnerable parts in their lives, not creating a church.

- It is about Jesus reaching out to people that everyone else counts as of no importance, rather than sitting in a room writing his gospel.

If there is anything entrusted to our care as Christian people, it is this idea of encounter. Through the encouragement we give to the people whom we meet, and in our own personal encounter, we lead others to make their own encounter with Christ.

Part of the joy of this New Year was, for the first time for me not for the rest of the family, but for the first time for me, in over twenty years, we shared New Year's Day physically. Now, nobody is diminishing the power of communication. Nobody is diminishing the power of the text messages from our children as they travel the globe, the e-mails at New Year or at Christmas from friends who we know are simply too far away to visit. Yet, there is no substitute for the encounter. Ask any grandparent. You may send as many photographs as you want, but there is no substitute for lifting the child. That is what incarnation is. It is God's encounter with us, the physical manifestation of being with us. God in his wisdom knew that nothing else would do.

So, do we have any resolutions as a Church? For our text, I want to go back to the Old Testament rather than the New Testament, and that wonderful passage in Isaiah, chapter 43. As is the case in much of the Bible, there is a powerful sense of realism. This is written by people whose feet are on the ground, but who want to have a faith in, and relationship with, that which they cannot see. However, they are realistic. They are not saying that this faith, this encounter, suddenly makes the world a rosy place. We know it does not.

Let us remind ourselves what Isaiah *did* say. *'This is what the Lord says, fear not for I have redeemed you. I have summoned you by name and you are mine.* Now that, in itself, would be a wonderful thing to take into this New Year, whatever it brings. Some of what the year has in store for us we know. There will be:

- ventures already in our diaries,
- anticipated work and family events,
- perhaps the challenge of new jobs or even a new home.

Besides these, there is much we do not know – and let us be grateful for that. I love it when people look at their horoscope. They do not want to know the future really. They do want to know only if it involves winning the lottery; but coping with the present is hard enough. Even the writer in Isaiah recognises that whatever we say, whatever we do, we know that for all of us the New Year will contain difficulties and sadness as every other year has.

So, the writer of Isaiah does not simply say: 'We will go with this nice little quotation from a calendar "I am with you"'. It recognises the challenges before us. *'When you pass through the waters, I will be with you, when you pass through the rivers, they will not sweep you away, when you walk through the fire, you will not be set ablaze since you are precious and honoured within my sight and because I love you.'* In other words, what the New Year holds for us is not us wondering if God is still there. It is not us wondering and agonising over whether God will support us. That is assured. That is his promise. That is God's resolution for us. The challenge for us is, when these things happen, to know that God is there and to encounter God in our sadness as well as our joy. I hope and pray that that will be true for you as individuals whatever this year brings:

- good and bad experiences we may have,
- whatever joys and sorrows may confront us,
- whatever anxieties we may have about the year ahead, over our families, over our health, over our job, our children.

He will be there when we need him. It is a matter of *when*, not if.

'When the time of trial comes I will be with you, when you're in the waters of the deep I will be there for you.' Now, as we all know, unlike holidays, you cannot book God in advance. How often have we felt his presence when we have really needed it? How often have we had that encounter when we least thought we would meet? So, for us, as Christian people, the glass is always half-full. This is the challenge to take to a world that seems to be preoccupied already with doom and gloom.

Whatever else we should be as Christians, whatever else we give to the world, whatever face we show, one thing we should never do is give up hope and reliance on God's promised presence with us. This was the advice from an elderly minister, whom I trained under and who taught me much. He told me: 'Challenge people, comfort people, forgive people, welcome people, but do not ever bore them. You have been entrusted with a message that is for the salvation of all.'

What we have been entrusted with is *not* something that will make people feel a bit better. It is for their salvation. Yet, before we do and see anything, God says: 'I have redeemed you'. It has already happened. It is not up to us to make it happen, but to rest in the fact that it has. So, I hope, as this year unfolds, we may live and worship in the presence of God. I hope that we may go from this place to be his people in the power of God and, more than anything else, in these frantic lives that we all lead, that we might know something of the peace of God in the time that lies before us.

May God's richest blessing be with you all in this coming year.

Amen.

Index of Biblical Texts